YOUR VA LOAN:
And How It Can Make You a Millionaire

By Phil Capron

*© 2019 Phil Capron
All Rights Reserved*

The information in this book is for informational and entertainment purposes only and does not constitute financial, accounting, or legal advice. By reading this book you agree to hold me harmless from any ramifications, financial or otherwise, that occur to you as a result of acting on information found on this book.

This book is dedicated to our brothers and sisters who gave their lives for our freedom. May we live lives worthy of their sacrifice.

Table of Contents

Table of Contents	7
Chapter One:	1
Why I'm Writing This Book	1
Chapter Two:	7
You're Not Special, And Neither Am I	7
Chapter Three:	21
How Can Real Estate Make You A Millionaire?	21
Chapter Four:	72
The VA Loan	72
Chapter Five:	95
Your VA Loan Team	95
Chapter Six:	113
What Am I Buying?	113
Chapter Seven:	140
Advanced Strategies for Your VA Loan	140
Chapter Eight:	148
Growing Your Portfolio and Achieving Financial Freedom	148
Chapter Nine:	159
Keep Your Grit	159
Chapter 10:	163

Your Big Why and Your Big Who	163
Postlogue:	173
Moving Forward	173

Phil Capron

Chapter One:

Why I'm Writing This Book

Did you enjoy sitting down to write a five-page paper in high school or college?

Yeah, me neither.

That's one of the reasons that this section ended up as Chapter One. I had to constantly refer back to it as a reference point as to why I was voluntarily subjecting myself to so much mental anguish. As the poster child for ADD, all of my high school five-pagers were written at the last possible minute; either late at night or early morning prior to when they were due. I'm dating myself here, but this was an archaic time prior to the advent of the energy drinks. I think most of my essays were written after a couple of Surge sodas (Do they still make that crap?).

Attempting to write a book is something altogether different. Don't get me wrong, I'm definitely highly caffeinated right now, but it's also 10:30 on a Friday night and I decided to stay in and work on this; not because I "have to," but because it's important.

Quitting and going out with my friends would certainly have been easier. Since you're reading this, I know that you're not a quitter, either.

In my life, I've changed course often, but not before seeing a goal through, or at least leaving it all out on the field. I'm hard-headed and stubborn by nature, but any latent "quit" in my being was washed away training in the chilly Pacific waters off of Coronado, CA, or burnt to a crisp in the mountains around Camp Pendleton by white-hot .50 cal. barrels that were on the verge of melting if one more can of 100 rounds was put through them. A lot has happened in the ten years since I was there training to become a Naval Special Warfare Combatant Craft Crewman (SWCC) in 2009. A lot of which inspired me to write this book.

I separated from active duty after four years of honorable service in 2012, but not by choice (more on that later). I felt like I was dead in the water and didn't know what to do. Retreating home with not much to show for myself wasn't an option, so I was determined to figure something out. I used my VA Loan in 2010 and purchased a four-bedroom, three-and-a-half bath house a block from the Chesapeake Bay beach and five minutes from the Naval Amphibious Base Little Creek where I was stationed. After moving in three of my SWCC buddies, it was kind of like Animal House... but the house occupants had bigger muscles and wore camouflage adorned with detachment patches, call signs, and blood types in lieu of Greek letters. Instinctively, I knew there was something to this real estate thing, and took an online course to become a real estate agent when we were out on an extended training trip in the middle of nowhere. I took the course for my own knowledge, but when I received the news that I was separating from the Navy, being a realtor seemed like a viable option to pursue as a new career.

What I really mean by "seemed like a viable option" is that I had nowhere else to turn. My back was against the wall and I had to make it work. I had a lot of life experience for a twenty-eight-year-old, and that experience along with 99 cents gets me a cup of coffee at McDonald's. What I lacked was financial success, and I wasn't prepared to retreat home to Baltimore without it.

By applying the tenacity and no-quit attitude exemplified in the Naval Special Warfare (NSW) community, I quickly rose through the ranks on the leaderboard at the monthly meetings for my real estate office, and was among the top tier of real estate agents for the entire area. Helping my buddies from my old command buy houses was a lot of fun! And I was good at it! And the pay wasn't bad! It wasn't until a wave of guys came to me to sell their houses that I realized how much malpractice occurs in the residential real estate industry, and how the VA Loan—which is an unbelievable tool—can actually be used as a double-edged sword against the service member. This realization planted the seed for this book. I'm not naive enough to think that I'm going to be able to help every Veteran, but I am going to be able to help SOME. And that's enough. I want to help guys like my bunkmate from bootcamp; we'll call him Michael.

It was our first real "meal" at Basic Training Command, Great Lakes, IL. We filed into the bright, fluorescent lit cafeteria single file, silent, and received whatever the convicts on work release plopped on our trays. Talking was forbidden. We sat, shoveled the substance provided down our throats, and filed out the way we came a few minutes later.

Back at our "compartment of the ship" we folded skivvies, shined boots, and swept up the "dust bunnies" from those wool blankets that may as well have been made from straight sandpaper.

The Navy was on a mission to transform the dozens of men in Division 418—who, the day before, were simple cake-eating civilians—into hardened warriors of the sea in eight short weeks. So far, they hadn't tested us physically to speak of, but they sure were stretching the limits of how far a man could go before being bored or annoyed to death. So, there we were, doing all of those mind-numbing tasks imposed on us by the Petty Officers and Chief commanding our Division.

I was trying to make conversation with my new friend, Michael. For lack of anything better to discuss, I made some off-handed remark about dinner that was less than complimentary. Michael said he really liked the food in Boot Camp. I couldn't believe what I was hearing.

"Why in the world would this guy like the food here?" I asked

he simply responded, "They have dessert here." Dessert? Who cares?

Then it hit me like a ton of bricks; "They have dessert here."

I joined the military late, at twenty-four years old. I'd been out in the world for six years, and had been living very well as a college student, NCAA Swimmer and Water Polo player, an ocean lifeguard during the summers, a drummer for a touring punk rock band, and immediately before joining the military, a professional poker player riding the wave of popularity Texas Hold Em' enjoyed in the mid-2000s. Dessert was never an issue for me as an adult. Nor was it a problem while growing up in an affluent suburb of Baltimore, MD, and attending an elite Catholic prep school.

I'd been some places and seen some things in my life to that point, but it never occurred to me that there were Americans who did without dessert not because beach season was around the corner, but because they couldn't afford it. They exist, and Michael was one. Fortunately, he escaped from the poverty-stricken little town in Alabama in which he was raised and would soon be a Sailor in the world's finest Navy.

The epic film "Full Metal Jacket" sums up the transition from civilian to military life quite well when the Drill Instructor goes on a tirade concluding with the line, "Here, you are all equally worthless." The prep school kid and the kid from rural Alabama who didn't get dessert growing up—and from what I could tell, that was among the least of his issues—were now equals. What you did before the military didn't matter, where you came from didn't guarantee success or failure. Sure, there are limits to how quickly you could advance in rank, and as in anything, there are politics, but I loved how the military gave everyone as close to a fresh start as possible.

Everyone reading this at one time signed their name on the dotted line on a blank check to the United States Government, for an amount up to and including your own life. That makes you among the best of us. Michael is among the best of us. I want as many of us as possible to achieve financial freedom, not just for ourselves, but for what we can do to continue to serve our country. I want as many of us as possible to return home and to teach the next generation in high school about history beyond the textbook; to coach little league and teach tenacity and teamwork; to start a Veteran Owned business and provide valuable goods and services to our economy; to work in our churches and faith based organizations, supporting their missions; and to run for office and affect real change in our country like Dan Crenshaw, Scott Taylor, Tulsi Gabbard, Pete Buttigieg and hundreds of others.

The missions listed above are all noble, but other than high office, they don't pay so well. My mission is to help create financial independence for as many of my brothers and sisters as possible, so they can pursue the missions that are important to them. There's nothing wrong with quietly raising a family; leaving everything behind, and sailing the Mediterranean on a catamaran; retiring and chasing a little white ball around; wrenching on cars in the garage all day, or whatever you dream up. I want you to have options.

It's no secret we don't make a ton of money at E-1, and truly, not that even that much at E-7. So many service members are worried about their GI Bill benefits, as they should be. It's a great program that provides a vehicle to better oneself, and I totally support that. The problem with only investing in yourself in this way, and spending a disproportionate amount of time working towards a degree with your GI Bill, is that it's just preparing you for another job. The famed stock trader, "The Oracle of Omaha," Warren Buffett summed it up very accurately when he said, "If you don't find a way to make money while you sleep, you'll work until you die." Spending a little time and effort on maximizing your VA Loan benefit will truly help you make money while you sleep.

How far you want to take this is up to you. We're all running different races, and what's right for me might not be right for you. I want you to have options. Before we proceed, know that these concepts—this process, this life—is simple... but it sure isn't easy. Especially not at the beginning.

I am going to challenge you; your thinking, your beliefs, your trajectory in life. My high school water polo coach always used to tell me, "Phil, men, like rivers, grow crooked when they follow the path of least resistance." I'm not suggesting that failing to own real estate makes you crooked. What I am saying is that passing up this opportunity to learn, grow, and start accumulating real wealth in a proven way puts you at risk of limiting your financial and time freedom in the future. The concepts illustrated in this book are never going to be the easiest road, but I believe they are the most rewarding when you look back on the one you've chosen. I hope that years from now, you can refer back to this, and that you'll agree!

Chapter Two:

You're Not Special, And Neither Am I

The human brain is an amazing thing. It's given us the creations of Mozart, Van Gogh, Da Vinci, and others. If you're more contemporary, think John Lennon, Jimmy Hendrix, Kurt Cobain, Dr. Dre… Christopher Columbus used it to discover the Americas. Elon Musk is using it to take us to Mars and beyond. All of these people were freaks because of how they were able to turn off many millennia worth of programming (or at least tell it to pipe down) and pursue passions, aspirations, and adventures way outside of the main stream. Perhaps this ability was a deciding factor in their success, when other artists, musicians, explorers, and innovators fell short.

The brain's primary objective is to keep us alive long enough to reproduce. Biologically, that's about it. All of this wonderful stuff we've figured out as humanity is just icing on the evolutionary cake.

I'm no genius: just ask any of my childhood teachers, or simply go through this book with a fine-tooth comb looking for syntax errors, run on sentences, and possibly a misspelling or two. (I'm sure my Mother, a retired Teacher, has already found several. And it's only chapter 1!) It's important that I get this fact out in the open: I'm not special. Because of how our brains are wired, after reading the next section, yours is going to label me. It will want to put me in a nice, neat little box and tell you all of the reasons that you and I are not the same. This defense mechanism will make you feel okay, or even good. You'll write me off as "different," "special," "privileged," or whatever else that awesome little supercomputer crammed in between your ears can come up with.

Since separating from active duty in late 2012, I have:

- Sold dozens of homes to VA Buyers and sold for VA Sellers
- Flipped dozens of homes, many of which ended up being sold to VA Buyers
- Completed over $25,000,000 in real estate transactions
- Acquired over 250 properties
- As of this writing, I control over $15,000,000 in real estate holdings

Currently, I spend my days coaching or mentoring people on various topics in the Real Estate Industry, and they pay me handsomely to do so. That's when I'm not surfing, skydiving, exploring New York City, travelling, going to concerts, or enjoying a leisurely walk with my Vizsla puppy named Dexter.

You see, because of leveraging the incredible vehicle of real estate, I've far surpassed my E-5 income simply by waking up every day. Those of us in the business like to call it "Mailbox Money." Also known as "Passive Income," it is the best kind of money. You do the work once (or at least the heavy lifting) and after that, it's evergreen. Your assets spin off income every month, and they build equity through multiple avenues every hour of every day. With passive income, there is no time clock to punch, it's always running. This book is an introduction to the concepts that have enabled me to replace my active duty income several times over. Because of the VA Loan, I've created a lifestyle of time freedom I couldn't even imagine when I was on active duty.

At this point, your reptilian brain should be kicking in and coming up with reasons why I was able to do what I just described, and why it's not in the cards for you. Again, I'm telling you, hand on the Bible, I'm not special. I am however, extremely privileged. I hit the jackpot with an amazing, supportive, and loving family.

My parents worked their asses off to give me and my sisters all of the best opportunities in life and made sure we were never in need of anything. We went on great vacations, attended summer camps, played instruments—you name it, we did it. With all of this support I received as a kid, I thrived!

I captained two sports in high school, played in the marching, jazz, concert, pit, and pep bands, and somehow still found time to play drums in a Ska/Punk garage band with my friends on the weekends. I squeaked by academically, and got into a good college where I was set to continue playing water polo and swimming as an NCAA athlete. Everything was looking great for eighteen-year old Phil!

I left home and headed for Ocean City, MD seeking employment as an ocean lifeguard. If I were medically diagnosed, I suspect it would be something along the lines of "he watched too much Baywatch as a youth." While not radically at first, things started to change once I was on my own.

At home, I had left high school as the Captain of a state championship team. Once I graduated to the NCAA, I rode the bench for the most part despite my best efforts. I thought I was pretty good at the drums. These music majors? They were a lot better. In high school, I did enough to get by academically., I loved learning but didn't perform well in a classroom setting. In college, my GPA started out at a number that didn't get me congratulated or yelled at when I went home for the holidays, and that was a good thing. After a little while, that started to slide as well. All of the sudden, out in the world I was failing at a lot of things I thought I was pretty good at. Not a fun feeling.

Then I saw a flyer one day while waiting to get into a Bio lab: "Drummer needed: punk, rock, alternative." I couldn't resist. I auditioned that weekend and went on to play well over 100 shows with that band, just about everywhere East of the Mississippi. Touring around the east coast with my buddies playing for anywhere between nobody and 500 people every night was a lot of fun, but unfortunately, it didn't pay particularly well. It seemed that we'd missed the ground-swell produced by bands like Green Day, Blink

182, and All Time Low. Tours cost money, and college kids tended not to have a lot of it, so I took up Texas Hold Em' Poker and strategically routed tours around casinos so I could stop in and play for a few hours; long enough to get gas money, a bite to eat, and if I ran well, enough money for a hotel instead of sleeping 3 wide in the back of the Suburban. Our smallest band member was our guitarist and singer, who was 6'1. It was tight. We were packed in like sardines, living off of Ramen and hot dogs—but we didn't want it any other way at the time.

As bands tend to do, we went our separate ways after being teased with a little radio time across a few East Coast stations and a handful of opening slots for headlining bands we idolized. So, at 23, I was on the hunt for what was next. Unfortunately, this was not before I'd prioritized the band over my studies and withdrawn from school as a senior. Hindsight being twenty-twenty, perhaps not the best decision. The year was 2007 and I was bandless and had done irreparable damage to my college career. My friends who had stayed in school were preparing to head out into the world and faced the worst job market in generations.

At that time, I had a decision to make: go back to school or get a job. Fortunately, after meeting my best friend and co-captain of our high school teams for a drink over the Thanksgiving holiday, I learned there was a third option. Don took a radically different path from my own after high school, attending the Naval Academy, being commissioned, ultimately earning his Trident, and becoming a leader at one of the elite east coast SEAL teams. He was always a hard worker, unbelievable athlete, and very smart, but something was different about him at this meeting, and I wanted in.

After a few beers and some talk about my options, I decided to enlist in the Navy and seek a contract to become a Special Warfare Combatant Craft Crewman (SWCC). It seemed like a logical fit, since I'd spent so much time on and around the ocean patrolling the beaches of Ocean City, MD, as a lifeguard. SWCC operate in coastal and riverine environments, working closely with the SEAL Teams and other SOCOM forces, so it sounded like a pretty good time to me.

Phil Capron

September of 2008, after one last summer at the beach to "train" (and by train I mean hang out with my friends, surf, get a tan, and also do a little PT and beach running), the time had come to board the plane bound for Chicago and the Navy Boot Camp at Great Lakes. Since I was one of the older guys, 24, I was put in charge of the other six recruits and entrusted to make sure they all made it to the bus in Chicago. Our flight got in early, and I had the idea to go have one last run at the food court before reporting, but was outvoted by the others who wanted to check in.

At the meeting place within the airport, we were made to sit in a line against the wall; an exhibit for the other travelers to gawk at as they headed for baggage claim. They confiscated my copy of Marcus Luttrell's "Lone Survivor," and like you'd suspect, weren't particularly nice to us in any way. As you may have guessed... no food court. My first lesson in leadership: it's not a democracy. Fortunately, they failed to find my iPod whose battery lasted for about two weeks and provided a little remnant of home after lights out every night. Navy Boot Camp didn't provide a whole lot of challenges physically, but I'm fairly certain one of their tactics was to see if they could bore us all to death.

Before I knew it, graduation day was upon us, and my fellow Seamen and I were shipped off to various places around the Fleet. For me, it was Coronado, CA., the home of Naval Special Warfare Basic Training Command. Unlike Boot Camp, we definitely were tested physically as well as mentally during SWCC school.

Long beach runs and grueling PT for hours on end took out a lot of victims from my class, but the most effective weapon wielded by the instructor cadre was the water. If you weren't comfortable in the water, or couldn't figure it out very quickly, your days in the NSW training pipeline were numbered. It was simply a matter of time. Because of my knowledge of the ocean as an avid surfer and beach lifeguard, and my background as a competitive swimmer and collegiate water polo player, the water was my refuge. I learned how to become an above-average runner.

At 6'4," PT has never been my strong suit, but being extremely competent in the water gave me a real advantage throughout training. I was resting while others thought they might actually drown. My roommate almost did.

During an evolution called "brick treads," which is exactly what it sounds like —treading water with a brick or two above your head—he fought the entire way down to the bottom of the pool, went limp, and one of the instructors manning the watch from the diving platform dove in to save him. Many didn't have the heart for that kind of performance, and quit while under a lot less duress.

I was surprised how many guys came back after a weekend of rest and DORed (dropped on request) before the first training evolution Monday morning. They couldn't focus on the target that was right in front of them… Instead, they compiled all of the targets into one insurmountable task. Some couldn't stand the cold, some couldn't navigate the water, some broke physically; but most of the quitters failed to master their minds.

Real estate has a lot of parallels with Special Ops training. Tactically, it's not particularly difficult; it's not rocket science. Success is reserved for those who can forgo the hot shower, reject the hot coffee the instructors are offering when you've been in and out of Pacific for hours on end, and see the mission through.

On a sunny San Diego afternoon, I graduated as one of the newest Naval Special Warfare Combatant Craft Crewmen alongside a bunch of badasses in SWCC Class 62. We had been whittled and chiseled from thousands of young men who inquired with a recruiter, to hundreds who made it to boot camp with their dream intact, to only a couple of dozens of hard-nosed men who survived the cauldron of SWCC school.

Proudly wearing our Naval Special Warfare Combatant Craft Crewman insignias, we headed to one of three SWCC Teams. I arrived at Naval Amphibious Base Little Creek in September of 2009, checking in to my first command, and feeling ten feet tall for being one of the few left standing to receive my SWCC warfare insignia and be assigned to a Team. Unfortunately, it was soon clear that my Navy career had peaked in Coronado.

Phil Capron

A few New Guys were picked to attend language school during our pre-deployment work up, and I was one. Instead of shooting, moving, and communicating, I was practicing vocabulary and conjugating verbs. Upon returning to my detachment, the other New Guys were light years ahead, and I failed to catch up.

On my second-to-last jump at free fall school—a night jump with full combat gear—I made an unforgivable safety error and was dropped from the course, which caused me to miss deployment. I spent the next year in Training Department facilitating exercises for Detachments heading out to various theatres and doing any work beneath those who were no longer New Guys.

Finally, new detachments were drafted and I was picked up for one with a great mission. I couldn't wait! Unfortunately, that Detachment Chief hated my guts and made my life a living hell. I can't remember the exact number, but he loved writing me counseling chits. I lost count after a dozen.

On a training trip in the deep south, I contracted some unknown virus that left me unconscious on the bathroom floor with a 105-degree fever, to be found by the rest of the guys when they returned to base after a Friday night in New Orleans. Eight days sick in quarters, delirious, unable to eat, and twenty pounds lighter, the fever broke and I went back out on patrol with the boys in the July sun. Unsurprisingly, I fell out during a patrol due to heat exhaustion in my weakened state—in front of the Commanding Officer, as if my past week hadn't been bad enough. I was at my breaking point, but was determined not to quit... even though it seemed like no matter what I did, it was never enough, or it was just flat wrong. I learned on that trip to never ask the question "how could this be any worse?" because the universe has a way of showing you in ways that you couldn't imagine.

Still weary from the fever that had incapacitated me for a week, cut down 10% of my body mass, and made me look like a pansy in front of my Commanding Officer, I made an error that haunted me for years.

We had completed another arduous day filled with lots of shooting, patrolling, and other tactical movements, and I was on my last legs. Loading up as the turret gunner of my vehicle, I had a particular routine: unclip my M-4 and place it behind me in the turret in order to avoid bashing my optics or laser on the vehicle while riding; make sure my M240 was good to go, then fix my eye protection and scarf to keep as much of the gravel and dust out of my orifices as possible.

The Humvee started rolling during step 1. I didn't think much of it and completed my routine. Once we were on the main road, the fresh air felt great and I knew that after cleaning all of our weapons, I had some much-needed dinner to devour. We pulled into our outpost, victorious—or so I thought. I looked behind me to grab my M4, and immediately, my stomach dropped like a faulty elevator straight to the pits of hell. It was gone.

I wished I had gone with my stomach, down into the earth, invisible to my teammates and the watchful eye of the instructor cadre facilitating our training. Being in the ground seemed preferable to the fate of the junior enlisted man who had just lost control of a fully automatic weapon on some patch of American soil on the ten-mile stretch between the range and our outpost. Quickly, I grabbed the driver of my vehicle, my fire team leader, and said "Bro, we've got to go back." Before I could explain, the Suburban with the instructor cadre pulled up and the lead instructor, a former Army ODA guy, hopped out with a grin like the damn Grinch that stole Christmas. And my rifle.

"Missing something, Capron?" he smirked.

Back in Virginia, standing at attention in my dress whites, in front of a whole mess of pissed off E-7s and up, was one of the lowest points in my life. Complete, total, and utter humiliation. I fancied myself to be a pretty tough customer at this point in my life, but I sure wasn't for those few seemingly endless hours of inquisition. The faces and the questions varied, but the theme of the day was, "Why are you such an unbelievable piece of shit?" If I had made one mistake, perhaps it would have gone a little different, but as previously mentioned, my immediate superior wrote me counseling chits like a NYC meter maid writes parking tickets. With that kind of paper trail, I didn't stand a chance.

Phil Capron

After what seemed like hours of inquisition, they'd determined I'd had enough and the E-8 presiding asked a final, patronizing question in the way of a statement. "What we're doing here… what we're trying to figure out, is… are you a broken leg? Or are you cancer? Do you know why?"

"Because a broken leg can be reset," I responded. Voice cracking. Tears streaming. A tough guy worthy of my community's heritage and the warfare device on my chest, I was not.

As for my career, I'd say it was all over, it just wasn't finished. The writing was on the wall, but in a language I didn't understand. So, I kept trying. I was assigned to Operations, where my daily duties included shredding and ensuring the proper disposal of Classified documents, sweeping, and general administrative duties in an amount that would make anyone who didn't choose an admin job want to puke. But hey, I had nobody to thank for my plight but myself. When opportunities presented themselves, I volunteered as support personnel for training trips and would do any job for a chance to get in the mix with my guys.

My opportunity came when one of my instructors from Coronado checked in as a Chief and was next in rotation for the next deployment cycle. Against all odds, and against the counsel of Team leadership, he drafted me from the manning board, and I was back at it. Back to doing my job as a Comms/Nav guy, bow gunner (boat), turret gunner (land), and a free fall parachutist. I had a great group of guys surrounding me and a strong, capable leader at the helm in my Chief. Life was golden.

Life WAS golden. And as Robert Frost rightly pointed out almost 100 years ago, "nothing gold can stay." We had made it through the entire pre-deployment training work-up as a team and we were performing exceptionally. Then we headed down south, to the same outpost where I'd gotten sick and lost my M4 over a year before. New detachment, new Phil—everything was going swimmingly.

It was the final exercise of our multi-week course, and our job was to exit a hard point we'd taken over, fight from the structure to our vehicles (which somehow arrive, empty, under enemy fire, about 25 yards from the structure), and egress. As turret gunner of vehicle #2, my job was the same as turret 1 and 3. Get the crew served weapons up ASAP and suppress the Opposition Force that was spewing paintballs and Submunitions our way, so we could get off the X. We moved from the building, covering one another, and bounding towards the convoy; and before long, I was inside the Humvee, popped up in my turret, loaded my 240 with blanks, and returned fire. I was the only turret to get online and return fire before we rolled.

Back at our outpost, we cleaned weapons and congratulated one another on completing the last major training block before deployment. Chief wanted to see me, so I followed him into the briefing room where members of the training cadre were waiting.

"You had a negligent discharge," one of the instructors said, matter of fact.

"What the hell are you talking about?" I retorted in disbelief.

"The blanks from the 240. You didn't have a clean shot at the OpFor and stopped firing when you realized it." Different instructor. Same matter of fact tone.

"I sure did. I stopped firing because one of the guys heading for vehicle 3 was entering from the contact side (the side the enemy is firing from, Air Force) and I didn't want to flag (cover him with my muzzle, Coast Guard) him."

In deja vu like fashion, I was back in Virginia preparing for another round with a bunch of high-ranking dudes, like a pack of dogs, using my ass as a chew toy. This time, however, I had no reason to be ashamed. I'd done it right, for an entire pre-deployment work-up. I was beginning to understand the language in which the writing on the wall was inscribed, and went on the offensive. I petitioned the Commanding Officer for an audience to plead my case, which was denied.

The Command Legal Officer gave me instructions regarding the "review board" I would be facing. He presented the evidence that would be used against me and gave me a copy, let me know there would be no witnesses against me, and invited me to make a written statement and to call witnesses to my defense as I saw fit. With two days to prepare, I got on the phone to see who would be willing to testify on my behalf, and got to writing.

I was fully prepared for this board, and was ready to knock it out of the park. When the five panelists heard what my witnesses had to say about the event in question and on my work ethic and character, I knew I would prevail. I was standing ready to answer any and all of their questions at 10:00 when it was scheduled to start. Ten o'clock came and passed, as did eleven, and I was getting nervous rather quickly. Finally, around 12:00, I was escorted down to the Chief's Mess where the board was being held.

"Recite the SWCC Creed," the man sitting in the center of the panel instructed.

Nervously, I read the Creed and performed a facing maneuver to turn back towards the panel of five. The man in the middle spoke again.

"Now this is just my opinion, but I've never heard the SWCC Creed read with such little enthusiasm, and I think that speaks volumes about your character. Ok! Let's begin!"

Shell shocked, frazzled, in disbelief of what I'd just heard, I began to answer their questions. I wondered where my witnesses and Air Ops were. Where's Doc? Where are the guys from my Detachment? Where are they? The writing on the wall was becoming even more clear, but I still couldn't quite make it out. My plan was to come in on offense, but I was on my heels from the word go. I stayed and fought; one man fighting for his career, against five who seemed to just be really enjoying their Friday afternoon before a much-needed weekend. Sometime after two, the man in the middle decided he'd heard enough and dismissed me; the fate of my military career hanging in the balance.

Completely and utterly dejected, I took off my uniform and started the drive home to Baltimore for a weekend with family. I replayed the day's events in my head, where were my witnesses? That question was really gnawing at me, so I picked up the phone to find out.

The first guy I called answered and I laid into him right off the bat asking him how he could leave me hanging like that. He quickly set me straight. He WAS there, so were the handful of others who gave me their word. They sat in the hall from 09:45 to 11:30, waiting to come in and answer my questions. That was what was supposed to happen, according to the Legal Officer. What actually happened is they were called in, one by one, and asked "Do you know Phil Capron?" to which each answered in the affirmative, waiting for a follow-on question, wondering where I was at my own board, and the next word they heard was "dismissed."

That revelation made my stomach turn, but the next, the reason why I was left waiting for two hours before arriving at my own board, was the final straw. I wasn't allowed in, because the panel of five had almost two hours with a surprise witness... my former Chief, the one who wrote me the scores of counseling chits. Blood boiling, I thanked my friend and ended the call. The writing on the wall was clear, finally.

IT'S NOT ABOUT YOU.

I was ordered to surrender my SWCC pin upon returning the following week. What I'd worked so hard to earn was now a thing of the past, and my dream of deploying alongside real heroes and having the opportunity to make a difference defending our nation would remain just that, a dream. Even though I could read the writing, it didn't make it easier. My entire purpose in life was stripped away. I was Special Boat Operator Second Class Phil Capron. I didn't know who Phil Capron was anymore without the job and rank in front.

It was hands-down the worst time in my life. I was dead in the water, set adrift in the open sea. I wondered why this was happening to me, and then I remembered the writing on the wall. As great as our military and individual units within it are, its sole purpose is the defense of our country. Period. Full stop. There is no fair; there is only mission accomplishment. That's it.

Once I truly realized it wasn't about me, I was able to heal and move on. Ultimately, the events of my fouled SWCC career happened FOR me, not TO me. Fortunately, I had enough time before separating from active duty to activate my real estate license and hit the ground running as soon as I was officially reverted to civilian status.

Why did I just share that incredibly humbling tale with you—that most of my friends and family haven't even heard? Coming full circle from the beginning of the chapter, it's critical that you understand that we are the same. If you were a shitbag, hey! So was I, and look at me now! If you are a rock star, soldier, sailor, or airman of the year... hey! If the shitbag can do it, so can you!

I'm being a little tongue in cheek here, because a shitbag I am not. In 2011, I'm not sure if I would have been able to look you in the eye and tell you that. But I know that some of you reading this who are still dealing with similar situations, though hopefully not as severe. Trust me, the limitations and judgement those in your command put upon you are not you. They need to put you in a box and label you; they need the big, ugly machine to keep working; they need to ensure mission accomplishment. As a great mentor of mine, Rock Thomas, the founder of the "I Am" movement, famously says "The words that follow I am, follow you." So, guard those labels jealously, and make sure it's you that's doing the labeling.

What you must understand is that the military is run by humans, and any organization run by humans is far from perfect, it's life. I forgive those in my command who did not treat me fairly. I understand why they did it. Their allegiance was to mission readiness; not the junior enlisted guy who didn't quite fit in.

I forgive myself for the mistakes I made and the areas in which I could have done more. Had I been a better operator, I wouldn't have been under the microscope to begin with. Again, while I wouldn't wish it on anyone, this chapter of my life happened FOR ME. My highest and best use was not serving as a SWCC. My mission is to help as many of my Brothers and Sisters achieve financial freedom through real estate, using this amazing VA Loan benefit as a launch pad, so that they may take care of themselves and their families post service.

With that in mind, you must seek opportunities to better yourself and provide for your goals and the security of your family. Mission first, team gear, your gear, then you. That was always our pecking order for tasks.

I implore you to not forget about you. That's why I'm thrilled and honored you're reading this book. Draw on your military experience, and use the muscle you've built of being tenacious in your endeavors. Erase "quit" from your list of possibilities. Put in the work to learn the concepts in this book, you've done a lot harder in your life, I know! Then, wielding your new weapon, the VA Loan:

GET TO WORK!

Chapter Three:

How Can Real Estate Make You A Millionaire?

If you're anything like me when I was in grade school, you're going to hate this answer. It's the dirtiest of four-letter words. It is... Math.

There are several tried and true tools that real estate harnesses in order to create massive wealth over time. It's no surprise that over 90% of millionaires in the United States achieved their success through real estate. It's not easy, but it is simple. It works!

Again, if you're like I was as a school kid, you're not going to like spending a ton of time on this, so let's break it down to its simplest form to illustrate the concepts. Then we'll progress from a crawl, to walk, to run, and then on the marathon and commitment to lifelong growth that generates financial freedom. Trust me, the dollar signs that are the light at the end of the tunnel are worth a little bit of discomfort on the front end. Also, we'll look at the stories of real veterans just like you and how they did it, as well as hypotheticals to illustrate the various concepts. Let's dig in!

When you purchase a piece of real estate, there are five forces that begin to work on your behalf. Like an iceberg, the majority of these forces lurk below the waterline...

Four of the forces cannot readily be seen. The first, which seems like an obvious necessity to everyone who started buying property after the 2008 financial crisis, is cash flow. In the early to mid-2000s, people were buying property using "speculation"; they were banking on future appreciation of the property and accepting negative cash flow while waiting for the property to appreciate (increase in value) enough to sell for a profit. As millions learned during that awful time, that is not a sound strategy. "Cash flow" is simply…

PROPERTY INCOME-PROPERTY EXPENSES = CASH FLOW

In order to have a viable investment, a property must generate enough income to cover its expenses and then some. That is Rule #1 in this business. Unless you are a sophisticated investor, with deep pockets and a very good reason for violating it, treat Rule #1 as gospel.

I know what you're thinking… "Wait! We're talking about VA Loans; they are not investment properties! I'm going to be living there!" Touché. Thank you for paying attention.

Recently, I was privileged to attend an event where Robert Helms from "The Real Estate Guys" radio show was the keynote speaker. He gave a presentation on exactly what real estate and money are and articulated concepts that I felt, but couldn't put my finger on. It was not recorded, so I'll paraphrase slightly from my notes.

The gist of what he said was that no human has ever been or will ever be economically disconnected from real estate. From the early cavemen to people like us purchasing homes with our VA Loans, to the homeless looking for the most accommodating underpass, we all chose or will choose the best housing that we can obtain with our available means. As a landlord myself, I know that tenants (renters) expect that the rent will go up every year. I make it a point not to disappoint them. Purchasing a home with a VA Loan makes you the tenant and the landlord; you can decide not to raise the rent on yourself every year! Let's see what that looks like over time:

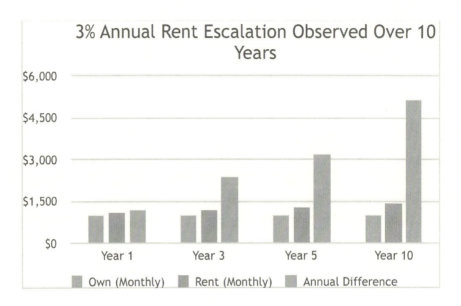

As you can see, over time this nontraditional "cash flow" grows to a sizeable amount of money saved. As the old saying goes, a penny saved is a penny earned. In this case, that's a lot of pennies! Perhaps you also noticed that owning was less expensive than renting from year 1, and there is good reason for this. Landlords aren't running charities, so our profit is almost like a "value added tax" on top of the true cost of that property. The value we add as landlords, is providing safe, clean, functional housing to the marketplace. While this may not be possible in every market, it is always our goal to purchase a property in a way that if you moved out the day after closing due to a PCS or other life circumstances, it would make money. If it doesn't, we are speculating, and we want to be investors, not speculators or gamblers betting on a better future based on forces outside of our control. We'll dig deeper into this concept later as it's one of the major considerations when analyzing a property. Here are a few other ideas to achieve cash flow while still living in the property:

House Hacking

- **Roommates/Houseshare**

- Your buddies rent directly from you instead of renting an apartment

  AirBnB
    - Rent a spare room anytime
    - Rent the entire space while on deployment

- **Garage storage**
  - Help your buddies avoid the hassle of a storage unit while they're on deployment

Cash Flow is Rule #1; it's the tip of the wealth building iceberg. It's what we can see peaking above the waterline; but what is lurking below the waterline is actually a much larger part of the whole than what we can see. There are four other forces that account for the majority of our wealth over time. All of the forces but one is malleable and can adjust based on market conditions, so we'll start with the core force, the one that doesn't change. Once we set it in motion, it's a snowball rolling downhill, getting larger and larger over the course of 30 years. This force is called Amortization.

Amortization

That's a scary sounding word, huh? According to Merriam Webster:

> ***Amortize*** *derives via Middle English and Anglo-French from Vulgar Latin admortire, meaning "to kill." The Latin noun mors ("death") is a root of "admortire"; it is related to our word murder, and it also gave us a word naming a kind of loan that is usually **amortized**: "mortgage."*

What are we killing? Debt. What are we giving birth to? Our financial freedom!

Phil Capron

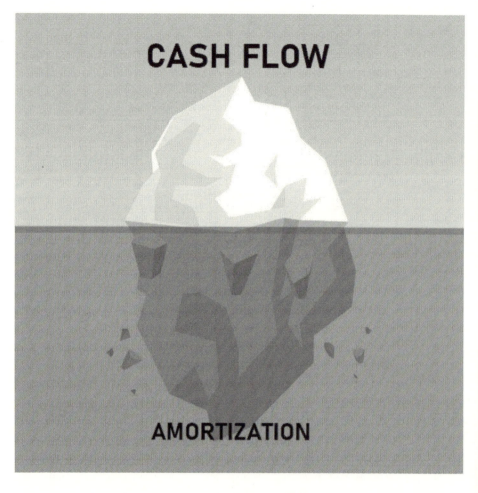

So, what IS "amortization"? Merriam-Webster defines it as:

> *"To pay off (an obligation, such as a mortgage) gradually usually by periodic payments of principal and interest."*

The difference between making a rent payment and making a mortgage payment is that a rent payment is paid to a landlord for the right to borrow (rent) their property for a period of time. A mortgage payment is paid to a bank for the right to borrow their money for a period of time, but this agreement is collateralized (secured) by YOUR property. As mentioned above, the "periodic payment" (monthly) to the bank is of "principal and interest."

Interest is the amount the bank collects in exchange for the privilege of borrowing their money. Isn't it better to borrow money for a property that belongs to you rather than pay money to borrow a property from someone else so that they may pay down their principal balance on the property? Principal is the total amount that the bank has lent on the property. Let's see what that looks like on a $100,000 property for simple math (spoiler alert: like landlords, banks are not charitable organizations, either!).

For this example, let's assume you've obtained a VA loan for 100% financing on a property, and that the purchase price, closing costs, the VA financing fee, and any other costs are neatly packaged in a $100,000 mortgage, on a 30-year term amortization, at a 5% interest rate. We will go into detail on the breakdown of loan terms in a subsequent chapter, so if your eyes are already crossing (I'm looking at you, Army), do not fear. We'll get there. For now, just take a look at the following:

- **Original Loan**: $100,000.00

- **Monthly Payment**: $536.82 (not including taxes and insurance)

- **Annual Payment amount**: $6,441.86

- **Total Payments over 30 Years**: $193,25.78

As noted previously, the bank certainly is not a charity. They receive *almost double* the original $100,000 loan amount over thirty years. As if that's not bad enough, let's take a look at the breakdown from year 1-30.

During the first full year of ownership, out of the $6,441.86 of payments, $4,929.22 is *interest!* Banks understand that people move, and the average life expectancy of a loan is only seven years, not thirty. With that in mind, they do not offer the consumer a loan that is weighted evenly across all thirty years. The interest is front loaded early in the loan term to enable the bank to make more money. Is that fair? I'm not touching that with a ten-foot pole. It is, however, reality. But now we know, and to quote a favorite childhood icon, "Knowing is half the battle." Here's a full breakdown of our example loan, over thirty years.

Warning: this table is 360 entries long, so it's the next couple pages.

Payment Date	Payment	Principal	Interest	Total Interest	Balance
Dec 2019	$536.82	$120.15	$416.67	$416.67	$99,879.85
Jan 2020	$536.82	$120.66	$416.17	$832.83	$99,759.19
Feb 2020	$536.82	$121.16	$415.66	$1,248.50	$99,638.03
Mar 2020	$536.82	$121.66	$415.16	$1,663.65	$99,516.37
Apr 2020	$536.82	$122.17	$414.65	$2,078.31	$99,394.20
May 2020	$536.82	$122.68	$414.14	$2,492.45	$99,271.52
Jun 2020	$536.82	$123.19	$413.63	$2,906.08	$99,148.33
Jul 2020	$536.82	$123.70	$413.12	$3,319.20	$99,024.62
Aug 2020	$536.82	$124.22	$412.60	$3,731.80	$98,900.41
Sep 2020	$536.82	$124.74	$412.09	$4,143.89	$98,775.67
Oct 2020	$536.82	$125.26	$411.57	$4,555.45	$98,650.41
Nov 2020	$536.82	$125.78	$411.04	$4,966.49	$98,524.63
Dec 2020	$536.82	$126.30	$410.52	$5,377.01	$98,398.33

Payment Date	Payment	Principal	Interest	Total Interest	Balance
Jan 2021	$536.82	$126.83	$409.99	$5,787.01	$98,271.50
Feb 2021	$536.82	$127.36	$409.46	$6,196.47	$98,144.15
Mar 2021	$536.82	$127.89	$408.93	$6,605.41	$98,016.26
Apr 2021	$536.82	$128.42	$408.40	$7,013.81	$97,887.84
May 2021	$536.82	$128.96	$407.87	$7,421.67	$97,758.88
Jun 2021	$536.82	$129.49	$407.33	$7,829.00	$97,629.39
Jul 2021	$536.82	$130.03	$406.79	$8,235.79	$97,499.36
Aug 2021	$536.82	$130.57	$406.25	$8,642.04	$97,368.78
Sep 2021	$536.82	$131.12	$405.70	$9,047.74	$97,237.66
Oct 2021	$536.82	$131.66	$405.16	$9,452.90	$97,106.00
Nov 2021	$536.82	$132.21	$404.61	$9,857.51	$96,973.79
Dec 2021	$536.82	$132.76	$404.06	$10,261.56	$96,841.02
Jan 2022	$536.82	$133.32	$403.50	$10,665.07	$96,707.71
Feb 2022	$536.82	$133.87	$402.95	$11,068.02	$96,573.83
Mar 2022	$536.82	$134.43	$402.39	$11,470.41	$96,439.40
Apr 2022	$536.82	$134.99	$401.83	$11,872.24	$96,304.41

Phil Capron

Payment Date	Payment	Principal	Interest	Total Interest	Balance
May 2022	$536.82	$135.55	$401.27	$12,273.51	$96,168.86
Jun 2022	$536.82	$136.12	$400.70	$12,674.21	$96,032.74
Jul 2022	$536.82	$136.69	$400.14	$13,074.35	$95,896.05
Aug 2022	$536.82	$137.25	$399.57	$13,473.91	$95,758.80
Sep 2022	$536.82	$137.83	$398.99	$13,872.91	$95,620.97
Oct 2022	$536.82	$138.40	$398.42	$14,271.33	$95,482.57
Nov 2022	$536.82	$138.98	$397.84	$14,669.17	$95,343.59
Dec 2022	$536.82	$139.56	$397.26	$15,066.44	$95,204.04
Jan 2023	$536.82	$140.14	$396.68	$15,463.12	$95,063.90
Feb 2023	$536.82	$140.72	$396.10	$15,859.22	$94,923.18
Mar 2023	$536.82	$141.31	$395.51	$16,254.73	$94,781.87
Apr 2023	$536.82	$141.90	$394.92	$16,649.66	$94,639.97
May 2023	$536.82	$142.49	$394.33	$17,043.99	$94,497.48
Jun 2023	$536.82	$143.08	$393.74	$17,437.73	$94,354.40
Jul 2023	$536.82	$143.68	$393.14	$17,830.87	$94,210.72
Aug 2023	$536.82	$144.28	$392.54	$18,223.42	$94,066.45

Payment Date	Payment	Principal	Interest	Total Interest	Balance
Sep 2023	$536.82	$144.88	$391.94	$18,615.36	$93,921.57
Oct 2023	$536.82	$145.48	$391.34	$19,006.70	$93,776.09
Nov 2023	$536.82	$146.09	$390.73	$19,397.44	$93,630.00
Dec 2023	$536.82	$146.70	$390.12	$19,787.56	$93,483.30
Jan 2024	$536.82	$147.31	$389.51	$20,177.08	$93,335.99
Feb 2024	$536.82	$147.92	$388.90	$20,565.98	$93,188.07
Mar 2024	$536.82	$148.54	$388.28	$20,954.26	$93,039.53
Apr 2024	$536.82	$149.16	$387.66	$21,341.92	$92,890.38
May 2024	$536.82	$149.78	$387.04	$21,728.97	$92,740.60
Jun 2024	$536.82	$150.40	$386.42	$22,115.39	$92,590.20
Jul 2024	$536.82	$151.03	$385.79	$22,501.18	$92,439.17
Aug 2024	$536.82	$151.66	$385.16	$22,886.34	$92,287.51
Sep 2024	$536.82	$152.29	$384.53	$23,270.87	$92,135.22
Oct 2024	$536.82	$152.92	$383.90	$23,654.77	$91,982.29
Nov 2024	$536.82	$153.56	$383.26	$24,038.03	$91,828.73
Dec 2024	$536.82	$154.20	$382.62	$24,420.65	$91,674.53

Payment Date	Payment	Principal	Interest	Total Interest	Balance
Jan 2025	$536.82	$154.84	$381.98	$24,802.63	$91,519.69
Feb 2025	$536.82	$155.49	$381.33	$25,183.96	$91,364.20
Mar 2025	$536.82	$156.14	$380.68	$25,564.64	$91,208.06
Apr 2025	$536.82	$156.79	$380.03	$25,944.68	$91,051.27
May 2025	$536.82	$157.44	$379.38	$26,324.06	$90,893.83
Jun 2025	$536.82	$158.10	$378.72	$26,702.78	$90,735.73
Jul 2025	$536.82	$158.76	$378.07	$27,080.85	$90,576.98
Aug 2025	$536.82	$159.42	$377.40	$27,458.25	$90,417.56
Sep 2025	$536.82	$160.08	$376.74	$27,834.99	$90,257.48
Oct 2025	$536.82	$160.75	$376.07	$28,211.06	$90,096.73
Nov 2025	$536.82	$161.42	$375.40	$28,586.47	$89,935.31
Dec 2025	$536.82	$162.09	$374.73	$28,961.20	$89,773.22
Jan 2026	$536.82	$162.77	$374.06	$29,335.25	$89,610.45
Feb 2026	$536.82	$163.44	$373.38	$29,708.63	$89,447.01
Mar 2026	$536.82	$164.13	$372.70	$30,081.32	$89,282.88
Apr 2026	$536.82	$164.81	$372.01	$30,453.34	$89,118.07

Payment Date	Payment	Principal	Interest	Total Interest	Balance
May 2026	$536.82	$165.50	$371.33	$30,824.66	$88,952.58
Jun 2026	$536.82	$166.19	$370.64	$31,195.30	$88,786.39
Jul 2026	$536.82	$166.88	$369.94	$31,565.24	$88,619.51
Aug 2026	$536.82	$167.57	$369.25	$31,934.49	$88,451.94
Sep 2026	$536.82	$168.27	$368.55	$32,303.04	$88,283.67
Oct 2026	$536.82	$168.97	$367.85	$32,670.89	$88,114.69
Nov 2026	$536.82	$169.68	$367.14	$33,038.03	$87,945.02
Dec 2026	$536.82	$170.38	$366.44	$33,404.47	$87,774.63
Jan 2027	$536.82	$171.09	$365.73	$33,770.20	$87,603.54
Feb 2027	$536.82	$171.81	$365.01	$34,135.21	$87,431.73
Mar 2027	$536.82	$172.52	$364.30	$34,499.51	$87,259.21
Apr 2027	$536.82	$173.24	$363.58	$34,863.09	$87,085.97
May 2027	$536.82	$173.96	$362.86	$35,225.95	$86,912.00
Jun 2027	$536.82	$174.69	$362.13	$35,588.08	$86,737.31
Jul 2027	$536.82	$175.42	$361.41	$35,949.49	$86,561.90
Aug 2027	$536.82	$176.15	$360.67	$36,310.16	$86,385.75

Payment Date	Payment	Principal	Interest	Total Interest	Balance
Sep 2027	$536.82	$176.88	$359.94	$36,670.10	$86,208.87
Oct 2027	$536.82	$177.62	$359.20	$37,029.31	$86,031.25
Nov 2027	$536.82	$178.36	$358.46	$37,387.77	$85,852.89
Dec 2027	$536.82	$179.10	$357.72	$37,745.49	$85,673.79
Jan 2028	$536.82	$179.85	$356.97	$38,102.46	$85,493.95
Feb 2028	$536.82	$180.60	$356.22	$38,458.69	$85,313.35
Mar 2028	$536.82	$181.35	$355.47	$38,814.16	$85,132.00
Apr 2028	$536.82	$182.10	$354.72	$39,168.88	$84,949.89
May 2028	$536.82	$182.86	$353.96	$39,522.84	$84,767.03
Jun 2028	$536.82	$183.63	$353.20	$39,876.03	$84,583.40
Jul 2028	$536.82	$184.39	$352.43	$40,228.46	$84,399.01
Aug 2028	$536.82	$185.16	$351.66	$40,580.13	$84,213.85
Sep 2028	$536.82	$185.93	$350.89	$40,931.02	$84,027.92
Oct 2028	$536.82	$186.71	$350.12	$41,281.13	$83,841.22
Nov 2028	$536.82	$187.48	$349.34	$41,630.47	$83,653.74
Dec 2028	$536.82	$188.26	$348.56	$41,979.03	$83,465.47

Payment Date	Payment	Principal	Interest	Total Interest	Balance
Jan 2029	$536.82	$189.05	$347.77	$42,326.80	$83,276.42
Feb 2029	$536.82	$189.84	$346.99	$42,673.79	$83,086.59
Mar 2029	$536.82	$190.63	$346.19	$43,019.98	$82,895.96
Apr 2029	$536.82	$191.42	$345.40	$43,365.38	$82,704.54
May 2029	$536.82	$192.22	$344.60	$43,709.98	$82,512.32
Jun 2029	$536.82	$193.02	$343.80	$44,053.78	$82,319.30
Jul 2029	$536.82	$193.82	$343.00	$44,396.78	$82,125.47
Aug 2029	$536.82	$194.63	$342.19	$44,738.97	$81,930.84
Sep 2029	$536.82	$195.44	$341.38	$45,080.35	$81,735.40
Oct 2029	$536.82	$196.26	$340.56	$45,420.91	$81,539.14
Nov 2029	$536.82	$197.08	$339.75	$45,760.66	$81,342.06
Dec 2029	$536.82	$197.90	$338.93	$46,099.58	$81,144.17
Jan 2030	$536.82	$198.72	$338.10	$46,437.69	$80,945.45
Feb 2030	$536.82	$199.55	$337.27	$46,774.96	$80,745.90
Mar 2030	$536.82	$200.38	$336.44	$47,111.40	$80,545.52
Apr 2030	$536.82	$201.22	$335.61	$47,447.01	$80,344.30

Payment Date	Payment	Principal	Interest	Total Interest	Balance
May 2030	$536.82	$202.05	$334.77	$47,781.77	$80,142.25
Jun 2030	$536.82	$202.90	$333.93	$48,115.70	$79,939.35
Jul 2030	$536.82	$203.74	$333.08	$48,448.78	$79,735.61
Aug 2030	$536.82	$204.59	$332.23	$48,781.01	$79,531.02
Sep 2030	$536.82	$205.44	$331.38	$49,112.39	$79,325.58
Oct 2030	$536.82	$206.30	$330.52	$49,442.91	$79,119.28
Nov 2030	$536.82	$207.16	$329.66	$49,772.58	$78,912.12
Dec 2030	$536.82	$208.02	$328.80	$50,101.38	$78,704.10
Jan 2031	$536.82	$208.89	$327.93	$50,429.31	$78,495.21
Feb 2031	$536.82	$209.76	$327.06	$50,756.38	$78,285.46
Mar 2031	$536.82	$210.63	$326.19	$51,082.57	$78,074.82
Apr 2031	$536.82	$211.51	$325.31	$51,407.88	$77,863.31
May 2031	$536.82	$212.39	$324.43	$51,732.31	$77,650.92
Jun 2031	$536.82	$213.28	$323.55	$52,055.85	$77,437.65
Jul 2031	$536.82	$214.16	$322.66	$52,378.51	$77,223.48
Aug 2031	$536.82	$215.06	$321.76	$52,700.27	$77,008.43

Payment Date	Payment	Principal	Interest	Total Interest	Balance
Sep 2031	$536.82	$215.95	$320.87	$53,021.14	$76,792.47
Oct 2031	$536.82	$216.85	$319.97	$53,341.11	$76,575.62
Nov 2031	$536.82	$217.76	$319.07	$53,660.18	$76,357.86
Dec 2031	$536.82	$218.66	$318.16	$53,978.33	$76,139.20
Jan 2032	$536.82	$219.57	$317.25	$54,295.58	$75,919.62
Feb 2032	$536.82	$220.49	$316.33	$54,611.91	$75,699.13
Mar 2032	$536.82	$221.41	$315.41	$54,927.33	$75,477.73
Apr 2032	$536.82	$222.33	$314.49	$55,241.82	$75,255.39
May 2032	$536.82	$223.26	$313.56	$55,555.38	$75,032.14
Jun 2032	$536.82	$224.19	$312.63	$55,868.01	$74,807.95
Jul 2032	$536.82	$225.12	$311.70	$56,179.71	$74,582.83
Aug 2032	$536.82	$226.06	$310.76	$56,490.48	$74,356.77
Sep 2032	$536.82	$227.00	$309.82	$56,800.30	$74,129.77
Oct 2032	$536.82	$227.95	$308.87	$57,109.17	$73,901.82
Nov 2032	$536.82	$228.90	$307.92	$57,417.09	$73,672.92
Dec 2032	$536.82	$229.85	$306.97	$57,724.06	$73,443.07

Payment Date	Payment	Principal	Interest	Total Interest	Balance
Jan 2033	$536.82	$230.81	$306.01	$58,030.08	$73,212.26
Feb 2033	$536.82	$231.77	$305.05	$58,335.13	$72,980.49
Mar 2033	$536.82	$232.74	$304.09	$58,639.21	$72,747.75
Apr 2033	$536.82	$233.71	$303.12	$58,942.33	$72,514.05
May 2033	$536.82	$234.68	$302.14	$59,244.47	$72,279.37
Jun 2033	$536.82	$235.66	$301.16	$59,545.64	$72,043.71
Jul 2033	$536.82	$236.64	$300.18	$59,845.82	$71,807.07
Aug 2033	$536.82	$237.63	$299.20	$60,145.01	$71,569.45
Sep 2033	$536.82	$238.62	$298.21	$60,443.22	$71,330.83
Oct 2033	$536.82	$239.61	$297.21	$60,740.43	$71,091.22
Nov 2033	$536.82	$240.61	$296.21	$61,036.64	$70,850.61
Dec 2033	$536.82	$241.61	$295.21	$61,331.86	$70,609.00
Jan 2034	$536.82	$242.62	$294.20	$61,626.06	$70,366.38
Feb 2034	$536.82	$243.63	$293.19	$61,919.25	$70,122.76
Mar 2034	$536.82	$244.64	$292.18	$62,211.43	$69,878.11
Apr 2034	$536.82	$245.66	$291.16	$62,502.59	$69,632.45

Payment Date	Payment	Principal	Interest	Total Interest	Balance
May 2034	$536.82	$246.69	$290.14	$62,792.73	$69,385.76
Jun 2034	$536.82	$247.71	$289.11	$63,081.83	$69,138.05
Jul 2034	$536.82	$248.75	$288.08	$63,369.91	$68,889.30
Aug 2034	$536.82	$249.78	$287.04	$63,656.95	$68,639.52
Sep 2034	$536.82	$250.82	$286.00	$63,942.94	$68,388.70
Oct 2034	$536.82	$251.87	$284.95	$64,227.90	$68,136.83
Nov 2034	$536.82	$252.92	$283.90	$64,511.80	$67,883.91
Dec 2034	$536.82	$253.97	$282.85	$64,794.65	$67,629.94
Jan 2035	$536.82	$255.03	$281.79	$65,076.44	$67,374.91
Feb 2035	$536.82	$256.09	$280.73	$65,357.17	$67,118.81
Mar 2035	$536.82	$257.16	$279.66	$65,636.83	$66,861.65
Apr 2035	$536.82	$258.23	$278.59	$65,915.42	$66,603.42
May 2035	$536.82	$259.31	$277.51	$66,192.94	$66,344.11
Jun 2035	$536.82	$260.39	$276.43	$66,469.37	$66,083.73
Jul 2035	$536.82	$261.47	$275.35	$66,744.72	$65,822.25
Aug 2035	$536.82	$262.56	$274.26	$67,018.98	$65,559.69

Payment Date	Payment	Principal	Interest	Total Interest	Balance
Sep 2035	$536.82	$263.66	$273.17	$67,292.14	$65,296.04
Oct 2035	$536.82	$264.75	$272.07	$67,564.21	$65,031.28
Nov 2035	$536.82	$265.86	$270.96	$67,835.17	$64,765.42
Dec 2035	$536.82	$266.97	$269.86	$68,105.03	$64,498.46
Jan 2036	$536.82	$268.08	$268.74	$68,373.77	$64,230.38
Feb 2036	$536.82	$269.20	$267.63	$68,641.40	$63,961.18
Mar 2036	$536.82	$270.32	$266.50	$68,907.91	$63,690.87
Apr 2036	$536.82	$271.44	$265.38	$69,173.28	$63,419.42
May 2036	$536.82	$272.57	$264.25	$69,437.53	$63,146.85
Jun 2036	$536.82	$273.71	$263.11	$69,700.64	$62,873.14
Jul 2036	$536.82	$274.85	$261.97	$69,962.62	$62,598.29
Aug 2036	$536.82	$276.00	$260.83	$70,223.44	$62,322.30
Sep 2036	$536.82	$277.15	$259.68	$70,483.12	$62,045.15
Oct 2036	$536.82	$278.30	$258.52	$70,741.64	$61,766.85
Nov 2036	$536.82	$279.46	$257.36	$70,999.00	$61,487.39
Dec 2036	$536.82	$280.62	$256.20	$71,255.20	$61,206.77

Payment Date	Payment	Principal	Interest	Total Interest	Balance
Jan 2037	$536.82	$281.79	$255.03	$71,510.23	$60,924.97
Feb 2037	$536.82	$282.97	$253.85	$71,764.08	$60,642.00
Mar 2037	$536.82	$284.15	$252.68	$72,016.76	$60,357.86
Apr 2037	$536.82	$285.33	$251.49	$72,268.25	$60,072.53
May 2037	$536.82	$286.52	$250.30	$72,518.55	$59,786.01
Jun 2037	$536.82	$287.71	$249.11	$72,767.66	$59,498.29
Jul 2037	$536.82	$288.91	$247.91	$73,015.57	$59,209.38
Aug 2037	$536.82	$290.12	$246.71	$73,262.27	$58,919.27
Sep 2037	$536.82	$291.32	$245.50	$73,507.77	$58,627.94
Oct 2037	$536.82	$292.54	$244.28	$73,752.05	$58,335.40
Nov 2037	$536.82	$293.76	$243.06	$73,995.12	$58,041.65
Dec 2037	$536.82	$294.98	$241.84	$74,236.96	$57,746.66
Jan 2038	$536.82	$296.21	$240.61	$74,477.57	$57,450.45
Feb 2038	$536.82	$297.44	$239.38	$74,716.95	$57,153.01
Mar 2038	$536.82	$298.68	$238.14	$74,955.08	$56,854.33
Apr 2038	$536.82	$299.93	$236.89	$75,191.98	$56,554.40

Payment Date	Payment	Principal	Interest	Total Interest	Balance
May 2038	$536.82	$301.18	$235.64	$75,427.62	$56,253.22
Jun 2038	$536.82	$302.43	$234.39	$75,662.01	$55,950.79
Jul 2038	$536.82	$303.69	$233.13	$75,895.14	$55,647.09
Aug 2038	$536.82	$304.96	$231.86	$76,127.00	$55,342.13
Sep 2038	$536.82	$306.23	$230.59	$76,357.59	$55,035.90
Oct 2038	$536.82	$307.51	$229.32	$76,586.91	$54,728.40
Nov 2038	$536.82	$308.79	$228.03	$76,814.94	$54,419.61
Dec 2038	$536.82	$310.07	$226.75	$77,041.69	$54,109.54
Jan 2039	$536.82	$311.37	$225.46	$77,267.15	$53,798.17
Feb 2039	$536.82	$312.66	$224.16	$77,491.31	$53,485.51
Mar 2039	$536.82	$313.97	$222.86	$77,714.16	$53,171.55
Apr 2039	$536.82	$315.27	$221.55	$77,935.71	$52,856.27
May 2039	$536.82	$316.59	$220.23	$78,155.94	$52,539.68
Jun 2039	$536.82	$317.91	$218.92	$78,374.86	$52,221.78
Jul 2039	$536.82	$319.23	$217.59	$78,592.45	$51,902.55
Aug 2039	$536.82	$320.56	$216.26	$78,808.71	$51,581.99

Payment Date	Payment	Principal	Interest	Total Interest	Balance
Sep 2039	$536.82	$321.90	$214.92	$79,023.64	$51,260.09
Oct 2039	$536.82	$323.24	$213.58	$79,237.22	$50,936.85
Nov 2039	$536.82	$324.58	$212.24	$79,449.46	$50,612.27
Dec 2039	$536.82	$325.94	$210.88	$79,660.34	$50,286.33
Jan 2040	$536.82	$327.30	$209.53	$79,869.87	$49,959.04
Feb 2040	$536.82	$328.66	$208.16	$80,078.03	$49,630.38
Mar 2040	$536.82	$330.03	$206.79	$80,284.82	$49,300.35
Apr 2040	$536.82	$331.40	$205.42	$80,490.24	$48,968.94
May 2040	$536.82	$332.78	$204.04	$80,694.28	$48,636.16
Jun 2040	$536.82	$334.17	$202.65	$80,896.93	$48,301.99
Jul 2040	$536.82	$335.56	$201.26	$81,098.19	$47,966.43
Aug 2040	$536.82	$336.96	$199.86	$81,298.05	$47,629.46
Sep 2040	$536.82	$338.37	$198.46	$81,496.50	$47,291.10
Oct 2040	$536.82	$339.78	$197.05	$81,693.55	$46,951.32
Nov 2040	$536.82	$341.19	$195.63	$81,889.18	$46,610.13
Dec 2040	$536.82	$342.61	$194.21	$82,083.39	$46,267.52

Phil Capron

Payment Date	Payment	Principal	Interest	Total Interest	Balance
Jan 2041	$536.82	$344.04	$192.78	$82,276.17	$45,923.48
Feb 2041	$536.82	$345.47	$191.35	$82,467.52	$45,578.01
Mar 2041	$536.82	$346.91	$189.91	$82,657.43	$45,231.09
Apr 2041	$536.82	$348.36	$188.46	$82,845.89	$44,882.73
May 2041	$536.82	$349.81	$187.01	$83,032.90	$44,532.92
Jun 2041	$536.82	$351.27	$185.55	$83,218.46	$44,181.66
Jul 2041	$536.82	$352.73	$184.09	$83,402.55	$43,828.92
Aug 2041	$536.82	$354.20	$182.62	$83,585.17	$43,474.72
Sep 2041	$536.82	$355.68	$181.14	$83,766.31	$43,119.05
Oct 2041	$536.82	$357.16	$179.66	$83,945.97	$42,761.89
Nov 2041	$536.82	$358.65	$178.17	$84,124.15	$42,403.24
Dec 2041	$536.82	$360.14	$176.68	$84,300.83	$42,043.10
Jan 2042	$536.82	$361.64	$175.18	$84,476.01	$41,681.46
Feb 2042	$536.82	$363.15	$173.67	$84,649.68	$41,318.31
Mar 2042	$536.82	$364.66	$172.16	$84,821.84	$40,953.65
Apr 2042	$536.82	$366.18	$170.64	$84,992.48	$40,587.46

Payment Date	Payment	Principal	Interest	Total Interest	Balance
May 2042	$536.82	$367.71	$169.11	$85,161.59	$40,219.76
Jun 2042	$536.82	$369.24	$167.58	$85,329.18	$39,850.52
Jul 2042	$536.82	$370.78	$166.04	$85,495.22	$39,479.74
Aug 2042	$536.82	$372.32	$164.50	$85,659.72	$39,107.42
Sep 2042	$536.82	$373.87	$162.95	$85,822.67	$38,733.54
Oct 2042	$536.82	$375.43	$161.39	$85,984.06	$38,358.11
Nov 2042	$536.82	$377.00	$159.83	$86,143.88	$37,981.11
Dec 2042	$536.82	$378.57	$158.25	$86,302.14	$37,602.55
Jan 2043	$536.82	$380.14	$156.68	$86,458.81	$37,222.40
Feb 2043	$536.82	$381.73	$155.09	$86,613.91	$36,840.68
Mar 2043	$536.82	$383.32	$153.50	$86,767.41	$36,457.36
Apr 2043	$536.82	$384.92	$151.91	$86,919.32	$36,072.44
May 2043	$536.82	$386.52	$150.30	$87,069.62	$35,685.92
Jun 2043	$536.82	$388.13	$148.69	$87,218.31	$35,297.79
Jul 2043	$536.82	$389.75	$147.07	$87,365.38	$34,908.04
Aug 2043	$536.82	$391.37	$145.45	$87,510.83	$34,516.67

Phil Capron

Payment Date	Payment	Principal	Interest	Total Interest	Balance
Sep 2043	$536.82	$393.00	$143.82	$87,654.65	$34,123.67
Oct 2043	$536.82	$394.64	$142.18	$87,796.84	$33,729.03
Nov 2043	$536.82	$396.28	$140.54	$87,937.37	$33,332.75
Dec 2043	$536.82	$397.94	$138.89	$88,076.26	$32,934.81
Jan 2044	$536.82	$399.59	$137.23	$88,213.49	$32,535.22
Feb 2044	$536.82	$401.26	$135.56	$88,349.05	$32,133.96
Mar 2044	$536.82	$402.93	$133.89	$88,482.94	$31,731.03
Apr 2044	$536.82	$404.61	$132.21	$88,615.16	$31,326.42
May 2044	$536.82	$406.29	$130.53	$88,745.68	$30,920.12
Jun 2044	$536.82	$407.99	$128.83	$88,874.52	$30,512.14
Jul 2044	$536.82	$409.69	$127.13	$89,001.65	$30,102.45
Aug 2044	$536.82	$411.39	$125.43	$89,127.08	$29,691.05
Sep 2044	$536.82	$413.11	$123.71	$89,250.79	$29,277.95
Oct 2044	$536.82	$414.83	$121.99	$89,372.78	$28,863.12
Nov 2044	$536.82	$416.56	$120.26	$89,493.04	$28,446.56
Dec 2044	$536.82	$418.29	$118.53	$89,611.57	$28,028.26

Payment Date	Payment	Principal	Interest	Total Interest	Balance
Jan 2045	$536.82	$420.04	$116.78	$89,728.36	$27,608.23
Feb 2045	$536.82	$421.79	$115.03	$89,843.39	$27,186.44
Mar 2045	$536.82	$423.54	$113.28	$89,956.67	$26,762.89
Apr 2045	$536.82	$425.31	$111.51	$90,068.18	$26,337.58
May 2045	$536.82	$427.08	$109.74	$90,177.92	$25,910.50
Jun 2045	$536.82	$428.86	$107.96	$90,285.88	$25,481.64
Jul 2045	$536.82	$430.65	$106.17	$90,392.05	$25,050.99
Aug 2045	$536.82	$432.44	$104.38	$90,496.43	$24,618.55
Sep 2045	$536.82	$434.24	$102.58	$90,599.01	$24,184.31
Oct 2045	$536.82	$436.05	$100.77	$90,699.78	$23,748.25
Nov 2045	$536.82	$437.87	$98.95	$90,798.73	$23,310.38
Dec 2045	$536.82	$439.70	$97.13	$90,895.85	$22,870.69
Jan 2046	$536.82	$441.53	$95.29	$90,991.15	$22,429.16
Feb 2046	$536.82	$443.37	$93.45	$91,084.60	$21,985.79
Mar 2046	$536.82	$445.21	$91.61	$91,176.21	$21,540.58
Apr 2046	$536.82	$447.07	$89.75	$91,265.96	$21,093.51

Phil Capron

Payment Date	Payment	Principal	Interest	Total Interest	Balance
May 2046	$536.82	$448.93	$87.89	$91,353.85	$20,644.58
Jun 2046	$536.82	$450.80	$86.02	$91,439.87	$20,193.77
Jul 2046	$536.82	$452.68	$84.14	$91,524.01	$19,741.09
Aug 2046	$536.82	$454.57	$82.25	$91,606.27	$19,286.53
Sep 2046	$536.82	$456.46	$80.36	$91,686.63	$18,830.07
Oct 2046	$536.82	$458.36	$78.46	$91,765.09	$18,371.70
Nov 2046	$536.82	$460.27	$76.55	$91,841.64	$17,911.43
Dec 2046	$536.82	$462.19	$74.63	$91,916.27	$17,449.24
Jan 2047	$536.82	$464.12	$72.71	$91,988.97	$16,985.12
Feb 2047	$536.82	$466.05	$70.77	$92,059.74	$16,519.07
Mar 2047	$536.82	$467.99	$68.83	$92,128.57	$16,051.08
Apr 2047	$536.82	$469.94	$66.88	$92,195.45	$15,581.14
May 2047	$536.82	$471.90	$64.92	$92,260.37	$15,109.24
Jun 2047	$536.82	$473.87	$62.96	$92,323.33	$14,635.37
Jul 2047	$536.82	$475.84	$60.98	$92,384.31	$14,159.53
Aug 2047	$536.82	$477.82	$59.00	$92,443.31	$13,681.71

Payment Date	Payment	Principal	Interest	Total Interest	Balance
Sep 2047	$536.82	$479.81	$57.01	$92,500.31	$13,201.89
Oct 2047	$536.82	$481.81	$55.01	$92,555.32	$12,720.08
Nov 2047	$536.82	$483.82	$53.00	$92,608.32	$12,236.26
Dec 2047	$536.82	$485.84	$50.98	$92,659.31	$11,750.42
Jan 2048	$536.82	$487.86	$48.96	$92,708.27	$11,262.56
Feb 2048	$536.82	$489.89	$46.93	$92,755.19	$10,772.66
Mar 2048	$536.82	$491.94	$44.89	$92,800.08	$10,280.73
Apr 2048	$536.82	$493.99	$42.84	$92,842.92	$9,786.74
May 2048	$536.82	$496.04	$40.78	$92,883.70	$9,290.70
Jun 2048	$536.82	$498.11	$38.71	$92,922.41	$8,792.59
Jul 2048	$536.82	$500.19	$36.64	$92,959.04	$8,292.40
Aug 2048	$536.82	$502.27	$34.55	$92,993.59	$7,790.13
Sep 2048	$536.82	$504.36	$32.46	$93,026.05	$7,285.77
Oct 2048	$536.82	$506.46	$30.36	$93,056.41	$6,779.31
Nov 2048	$536.82	$508.57	$28.25	$93,084.66	$6,270.73
Dec 2048	$536.82	$510.69	$26.13	$93,110.79	$5,760.04
Jan 2049	$536.82	$512.82	$24.00	$93,134.79	$5,247.22
Feb 2049	$536.82	$514.96	$21.86	$93,156.65	$4,732.26
Mar 2049	$536.82	$517.10	$19.72	$93,176.37	$4,215.16
Apr 2049	$536.82	$519.26	$17.56	$93,193.93	$3,695.90
May 2049	$536.82	$521.42	$15.40	$93,209.33	$3,174.47
Jun 2049	$536.82	$523.59	$13.23	$93,222.56	$2,650.88

Payment Date	Payment	Principal	Interest	Total Interest	Balance
Jul 2049	$536.82	$525.78	$11.05	$93,233.60	$2,125.10
Aug 2049	$536.82	$527.97	$8.85	$93,242.46	$1,597.14
Sep 2049	$536.82	$530.17	$6.65	$93,249.11	$1,066.97
Oct 2049	$536.82	$532.38	$4.45	$93,253.56	$534.59
Nov 2049	**$536.82**	**$534.59**	**$2.23**	**$93,255.78**	**$0.00**

Let's consider what this means to you, the owner, over time. If you hold this hypothetical property for ten years—Don't tell me that's too long to think about if you're considering making the military a career, you ARE thinking that far ahead—you've "earned" $17,500 over ten years simply by making your payments. Not terribly exciting, but not bad either considering much of that time someone ELSE will be putting money into that forced savings account on your behalf. Or as previously noted, you are receiving that amount by occupying the property yourself as well as enjoying "rent control" when your buddies' rent is going up every year. At fifteen years, and it becomes over $30,000. At year twenty, it's just shy of $50,000. Real estate isn't a way to get rich quick; it is a vehicle to become incredibly wealthy over time.

I know what you're thinking. The numbers above seem like a lot of work for not a ton of money. You're not wrong. The only thing we'll see right off the bat on a monthly basis with the purchase of a rental property (or in this case, a primary residence that we've vacated and has become a rental property) is the "cash flow." Cash flow is simply rent received minus expenses (mortgage, taxes, insurance, property manager, repairs, and so on). Cash flow is the tip of the iceberg.

As mentioned previously, we are seeking properties that will cash flow from Day 1 if we were to vacate and rent them at fair market value. Most of the mass of the iceberg is actually below the waterline. What I mean by that, is that you don't see the money immediately as you do with cash flow (the only force that's above the water line). Amortization, or principal paydown, is the only force that is not subjective or susceptible to market conditions. It's just math. Once the monthly payments commence, the gained equity can be easily tracked on an amortization table.

Go to www.yourvaloanandhowitcanmakeyouamillionaire.com to plug in your specific information and track your equity! Cash Flow and Amortization are amazing, but there are other forces at play which will make you money over time through your real estate investment, the most controversial of which is called Appreciation. If your parents or anyone you know purchased properties in the early to mid-2000's they either saw the best or worst of the forces of appreciation at work.

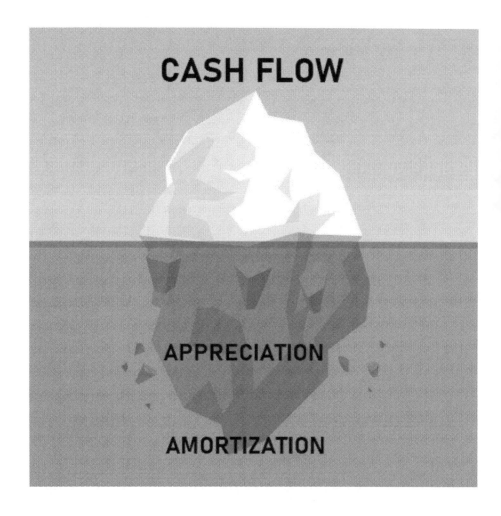

Appreciation

Simply put, appreciation is the gradual increase in the price of an item over time. In this case, we are talking about real property in the United States, and fortunately there is a lot of data around the appreciation of home prices over the years. Nobody has a crystal ball, but if we did, perhaps the 2008 real estate centric crisis would have been avoided. However, due to lending controls and a strong national economy, it is reasonable to project a certain level of appreciation in real estate values over a long enough timeline.

People got themselves in trouble in the mid-2000s when they were making real estate purchases ONLY on the hope of future appreciation and not on solid buying criteria and fundamentals. Others didn't buy additional property, but used their existing home like a piggy bank for liabilities like boats, cars, electronics, or vacations. They incurred additional debt and spent it on things that didn't make them additional income. As they learned, doing so is not a pathway to financial freedom. However, over time, appreciation does happen; though depending on it on a short timeline is a recipe for disaster.

Appreciation as a historical market force is too large to ignore, so we will discuss it here, and we will use conservative projections looking forward. Professional real estate investors like myself and those in my circles describe appreciation as "the icing on the cake." The other advantages to buying real property make up the actual cake. We know that over a long enough time horizon, we will enjoy some degree of appreciation. But to avoid the miserable fate of so many in 2008, we purchase on solid fundamentals right now. Let's take a look at historical data in order to apply some context to this concept.

The Census Bureau released a report that stated prices of homes increased 5.4% annually between 1963 and 2008. A similar finding from the National Association of Realtors found almost identical annual appreciation for the same period.

I'm sure you've heard the old adage "location, location, location" and that is always an important consideration when discussing real estate. When making appreciation projections, it's no different. Demographics are changing, politics are changing, economics are changing. Real estate markets are hyper local. A hip part of town might appreciate at double the rate of a tired neighborhood that's in decline. We'll discuss markets in excruciating detail in subsequent chapters, so for now let's assume a 3% annual appreciation to illustrate the power of this concept.

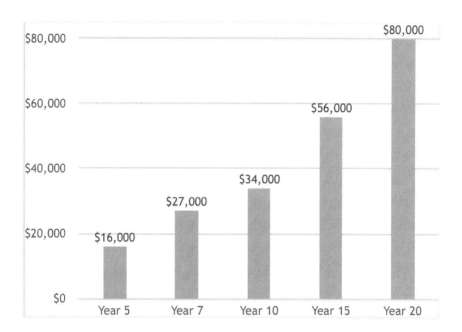

Again, we don't count on appreciation. It's the icing on a delicious, wealth building cake. However, over a reasonable hold period (10 years plus), based on past trends, we can assume that we will enjoy some appreciation. Let's take a look at the next way that real estate can create fantastic wealth for those who harness its awesome power.

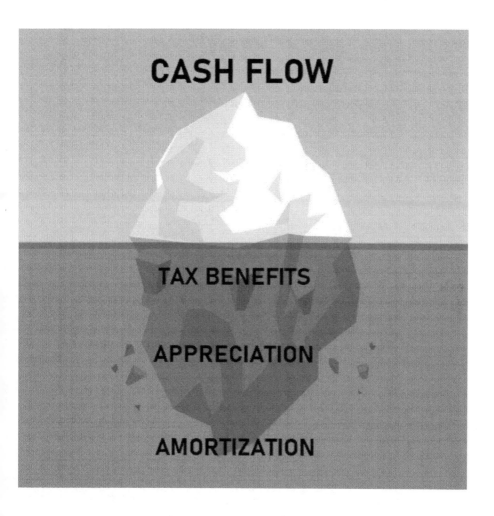

Tax Benefits

Did you know that most people work from January to May every year just to pay their taxes for the year? Depending on your tax bracket and the constant revision of the tax code, that amount will be different for everyone, so please consult your CPA. Here are a few great tax advantages associated with owning real estate based on the current laws as of this writing.

Phil Capron

Mortgage Interest & Municipal Tax Deduction

At the end of the year, your lender, ABC Bank or whomever, will send you an IRS form 1098. Kind of like the military, they have a form and acronym for just about everything. The 1098 itemizes the interest (remember that massive percentage of your monthly payment that the bank collects for the right to use their money?) as well as taxes escrowed to the city government on your home. Both of those items are deductible on your federal taxes, and the 1098 is what shows how much you may deduct. Tax planning is beyond the scope of this book, but here is a quick example.

Please consult your CPA (not an online or base tax preparer) for your unique situation. We'll discuss the CPA as a valued member of your wealth building team later, but if you're planning on ignoring my advice, I implore you to reconsider trying to save a couple hundred bucks by doing it yourself, online, or on base, and instead, to hire a professional who will best advise you on how to legally mitigate your largest annual expense! We are not cheating; we are simply making sure we understand the law as written and using it in a way that is best for us and our families. Here's that example:

Mortgage Interest Year 1: $4,929.22

Let's assume your tax bracket is 20%.

$4,929.22 x 0.2(20%) = $985.84

Your tax bracket and this interest would generate a tax liability decrease of *$985.84.*

Again, paying a professional two hundred bucks to navigate this necessary evil of American society will generate just shy of five times return on investment just on my back of the napkin example—not to mention reclaiming a few hours of your valuable time, and perhaps a little sanity, too.

The Tax & Jobs Act of 2017 established a generous "standard deduction" to simplify taxes for many Americans. If you are not a high-income earner, it will likely make sense to use the standard deduction. However, if you decide to really go for it with real estate as a means to achieve financial freedom, you will be acquiring a lot more in property than a $100,000 property that you live in.

As your financial position evolves, so will your tax liability and strategy. At a certain point, it will make sense to start itemizing using the concept outlined above. This will be a personal decision you should make with the expert counsel of a CPA. Even if itemizing deductions for your real estate isn't in the cards for you right now, there are other great money saving tools available to you now that you are a property owner.

Selling Your Home

These days, I'm in the business of being a real estate buyer, not a real estate seller (yes, I have flipped a lot of houses over the years, and I wish I still had all of them!). Everyone's situation and goals are different, so perhaps you have a different outlook about selling real estate. Maybe you'll decide against following the system of holding real estate for the long-term. Maybe a life event occurred that forced you to sell. Perhaps you are taking advantage of a lucky (or skillful) rapid increase in value of your property. Great! Everyone is on a different journey and I'm not judging.

No matter why you're selling, there is a significant tax advantage available for homeowners who have lived in the home for at least two of the last five years. If you meet that test, you may sell the property and not pay taxes on the first $250,000 of "capital gain," AKA profit, if you're a single person, or the first $500,000 of capital gain if you are married. Pretty great, right?

What would you do with an extra quarter of a million dollars? Several of my friends who purchased well in rapidly appreciating markets over the past decade or so are facing that fortuitous situation as I write this. I'd be lying if I said I wasn't a little jealous of my buddies who stayed in San Diego after graduation from SWCC school and purchased property there! The windfall my friends are enjoying wasn't planned, and in many cases, they got very lucky.

If you are committed to following the process outlined in this book, we can take a lot of the luck out of it and make our properties profitable regardless of "getting lucky." No matter what the cause of the equity in your property is—amortization, appreciation, or a combination of the two -you are looking at a potentially significant amount of money that you can enjoy tax free!

Another way you can avoid paying taxes and roll your sales proceeds into the next asset is called a 1031 Exchange.

1031 Tax Deferred Exchange

If you've occupied the home for two of the last five years as discussed above, you can take the gain (up to $250,000 single or $500,000 married) and do with it what you wish. Let's say that you purchased this property a long time ago, perhaps it was your first VA Loan purchase as a young service member, and you haven't lived there to qualify from the exemption above. Is there anything that can be done to mitigate your tax burden? There is, and it's called the 1031 Tax Deferred Exchange. Basically, what this option allows is for the profit (capital gain) on the sale of a property to be rolled into the down payment of a new property. Entire books have been written on the subject, so at risk of starting to sound like a broken record: consult your trusted CPA for guidance if you'd like to explore this strategy. Let's look at a quick, simple example:

You purchased a home using your VA Loan in 2004 for $150,000. You've paid off $50,000 of the mortgage balance, and despite the looming crash of 2008, you purchased in a great area and have enjoyed solid appreciation over the 15-yearterm and the current market value is $250,000. You moved out in 2008 and have been keeping it as a rental property since. You could sell and pay taxes on the $125,000 approximate profit (I've taken out 10% in fees to sell the property). Or, you could employ a 1031 Tax Deferred Exchange. In order to do so, you will have to identify a "like kind" (similar) property within forty-five days, work closely with a qualified 1031 Exchange company and your accountant, and close on the property within 180 days of selling the first property. Why would you want to do this other than deferring the capital gain?

Let's say you purchase a four-unit apartment building for $500,000 using the $125,000 gain as a down payment. Now you have started the process of

Amortization again, this time on a much more valuable piece of property. Cash flow should be much better on the quadruplex than on the single house, even if the ratio of rent to cost remains the same, the quadruplex is twice the price!

Additionally, you're putting $125,000, or 25% down, which means your mortgage is only $375,000 which allows for more cash flow than if the entire $500,000 was mortgaged. Ultimately, the monthly cash flow is what we seek to achieve financial freedom.

At a certain point, once it surpasses the amount needed to pay our monthly bills and afford the lifestyle you desire, you've made it. You're financially free. The 1031 Tax Deferred Exchange is a powerful tool you can use on your journey.

Cash Out Refinance

The VA allows Veterans to "Cash Out Refi" on their primary residence, whether that is currently owned with a VA Loan or some other loan product, or free and clear with no underlying mortgage. This product will include a lot of the same kinds of documentation needed for an initial VA Loan, but the result can make the juice worth the squeeze. Unlike conventional lenders that will only allow refinance up to 80% of the property's value, at most, the VA allows Veterans to refinance up to 100% of the property's appraised value.

Let's say you purchased a property using your VA Loan for $150,000 ten years ago and have enjoyed $30,000 of amortization (principal paydown), and the current market value of the house is $200,000. Only $120,000 is remaining on the previous mortgage. That's a difference of $80,000!

Again, this is TAX FREE money! It is important not to "over leverage" yourself. What I mean by that is, if your monthly payment was a stretch for you to afford on the $150,000 mortgage, the addition of another $50,000 in debt might make the payment uncomfortable for you. That's over leveraging. If you are reinvesting the proceeds into additional property (and thus, additional cash flow and other advantages long-term) it might make sense to stretch a bit. If your intention is to buy a new Tesla with the cash, that's probably not the optimal use of the cash out refi proceeds.

I'm doing my best to not get too far into the weeds on concepts that are more academic or regulatory in nature, because your team of professionals will be advising you on them, and regulations are constantly changing in the case of tax law and customs and fees are always ebbing and flowing in the case of real estate transaction and lender fees and structures. However, this is a concept worth exploring and explaining in further detail.

Your VA Loan, a Cash Out Refinance, or any other loan is actually a "debt" against you from an accounting perspective and in the eyes of the IRS. How can that be in the case of a Cash Out Refi? You're getting money, potentially a lot of it, back at closing. Simply put, even though you're signing on the dotted line and receiving money, you still owe the entirety of the new debt. In the case of our example, $200,000. So far, we've covered some pretty cool mechanisms to mitigate our tax liability and put more money in our pockets. There is one more tax advantage that puts real estate—which is already a fantastic tax mitigation vehicle—in a class of its own.

Depreciation

We've all got a crazy cousin Bill, or uncle Steve, or a friend from the old neighborhood who has a horror story about how they or someone they know (these stories get passed around like urban legends) lost in real estate. The air conditioner failed, the refrigerator quit, a pipe burst in the winter, whatever. I've had all of those things happen and then some. Their stories are all the same, only the names change. We'll dive deeper into this later, but there are some people who should not buy a house.

Spoiler alert: if you can't withstand a couple thousand-dollar expenses while the insurance processes your claim (in the case of a burst pipe, or another legitimately large expense), you should not be buying a house. The silver lining when an event like this eventually happens (if you own a property long enough, and something will happen), is that these expenses are what's called

"Capital Expenditures" or "CapEx," if you want to sound like you know what you're talking about.

At the end of the year, you can report 100% of your CapEx to your accountant and that amount will show up as a deduction on your taxes as "100% Bonus Depreciation." Additionally, a certain percentage of the entire property can be written off as regular or "straight line" depreciation. This means that every stick, brick, light switch, piece of drywall, and shred of carpet is depreciated from the time of purchase out to 27.5 years later, at which time those items will be "fully depreciated." Tax law constantly evolves, so consult with your CPA to see if it makes sense to write off any depreciation on your property, whether CapEx or straight line. Again, if your accountant determines you would benefit most from taking the standard deduction, it might not apply to you, yet.

I purchased an apartment building with three partners last year and it illustrates why you should not discount the value of Depreciation as your real estate portfolio grows. We purchased the property for just under $2,000,000 and after our accountant was finished with his analysis of the depreciation, each partner received a K1 (IRS form itemizing depreciation on real property) in the amount of $93,000. What that means is that I was able to reduce my income for that year by $93,000. Let's say that my income for the year was $250,000. Subtracting my K1 for that apartment building leaves my income for the year at $157,000, not $250,000. If I paid taxes on my entire income of $250,000 in the 2nd highest tax bracket (35%) I would owe $87,500. Because of my K1, my income is lower and I pay taxes on that amount. $157,000 x 35% = $54,950 which is a savings of $32,550! But wait, there's more. My new income of $157,000 is actually two tax brackets lower, which has an effective rate of 24%. $157,000 x 24% = $37,680.

Factoring in the reduction in income, as well as the change in tax bracket, the K1 and depreciation enclosed within saves me $49,820! Yes, you read that right. Just under $50,000 in tax mitigation in this example.

In order to receive that preferential treatment like I did, you must be a "real estate professional," which basically means you spend the majority of your time on real estate and you are active in the management of your real estate holdings. If you are not a real estate professional, your K1 passive losses can only offset your passive income. Consult your CPA with questions about depreciation and passive losses. I simply share this example to show you what is possible in this business, depending on how far you want to take it.

If you're like me, taxes probably aren't your favorite subject. I hear you. Fortunately, I've been exposed to great mentors who have changed my mindset about taxes, and it's my intention to pass what I've learned on to you. I used to fear taxes, but now I love them! I hope my bill is the biggest ever this year. Why? With the power of Depreciation, 1031 Exchange, and Cash Out Refi working for me… if I have a big bill, it means that I'm making gobs and gobs of money.

Finally, let's take a look at arguably the most important metric when dealing in real property: cash flow. It's the tip of the iceberg and Rule #1, but it's also the most obvious, which is why I chose to address it last.

Cash Flow

Robert Kiyosaki (a Vietnam Marine Pilot) is famously quoted as saying, "Your home is not an asset." This comment drew fire from all of the talking heads and financial gurus of the day in the 90s and 2000s. I don't want to saying Kiyosaki had the last laugh, because there was nothing funny about what happened in the financial crisis of 2008.

So many homes broken, lives shattered, and a mind-boggling amount of treasure flushed down the toilet. All because people were using their homes as piggy banks, and the good times were going to continue forever. Or so they thought.

It seems crazy to imagine knowing what we know now, but apparently people were buying properties in the mid-2000s with no regard to whether the purchaser could make the mortgage payments as promised, or if the property could actually break even, or ideally "cash flow" at a fair market rental rate in the event the owner were to vacate the property. A great movie covering these events that really breaks it down in a way anyone can understand is "The Big Short."

You know the landlord you've been paying every month who won't let you make the place you're staying feel like home by making improvements? The one who lines their pocket every month because your rent is significantly higher than their mortgage payment? The one who ensures your rent goes up every year, like clockwork? It's time to tell them "no more."

Once you purchase your home with your VA Loan, you lock your "rent" in for the next thirty years, if you so desire. I consider that to be a form of cash flow, as your mortgage will be less than that of a comparable property on the rental market (assuming you follow the system and buy your property correctly).

So, what is Cash Flow once you move out of your house? My definition of Cash Flow pertaining to a rental property is:

Cash Flow = Rent-Mortgage, Taxes, Insurance, and operational expenses

For Example:

Rent	$1,000.00
Mortgage	-$600.00
Taxes	-$50.00
Insurance	-$50.00
Property Manager	-$100.00
Maintenance	-$100.00
TOTAL CASH FLOW	**$100.00**

Those are all monthly numbers, so you end up with $1,200 in profit over the course of the year.

Everyone has a different risk tolerance and investment strategy, but if I encountered somebody, particularly someone new to real estate, who told me "I'm going to buy this property, I can't rent it for at LEAST the mortgage payment in today's market, but it's going to make a good investment" I would do everything I can to implore them to reconsider. In real estate, as in life, there is a lot you don't know that you don't know. If you purchase a property that has no ability to make you money AS-IS, you're setting yourself up for failure.

Now that we've introduced the wealth building forces that will begin working on your behalf as soon as you purchase a piece of America, let's tally up our assumptions based on our hypothetical example of a $100,000 purchase and see what that looks like over time.

Let's assume you're a young E-5 and purchase your first property with four or five years in, I think it's safe to assume you'd be happy to have a $116,967 bonus waiting for you as you transition out after twenty years of honorable service. Perhaps others read that and are thinking "Hey! Isn't this book *Your VA Loan: and how it can make you a millionaire?*" You're both right.

Receiving over a hundred grand for something you did once as a young E-5 is sweet, but it's not $1,000,000 sweet. How do we do that? Sorry, Army, it's back to Math again. The days of picking up decent properties for $100,000 have gone the way of the Do-Do bird in most markets. What's great about that? As we increase the price point and thus the amount of real estate we acquire, the forces discussed in this chapter conspire even more diligently to make us extremely wealthy over time. Let's take a look at a reasonable price point—$250,000—as well as a couple that might be more of a stretch depending on your market, but can be attained with multiple purchases, $500,000 and $1,000,000. We'll use the same assumptions as our example:

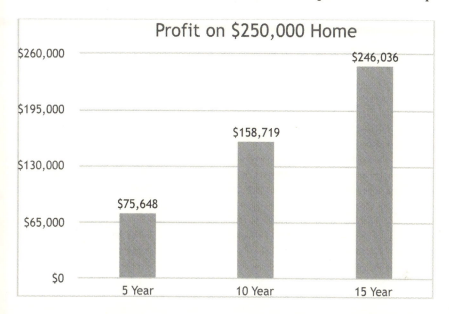

A quarter of a million dollars over fifteen years! What could you do with that money at retirement? Please don't say Ferrari... Lamborghini... Aston Martin... or the like. Trust me, I want you to have nice things, too. But we need to put in a little more work and get the real estate snowball rolling downhill before we hemorrhage money like that, though.

For a retirement gig, would you like to buy a catamaran and cruise around the Caribbean with your sweetheart? You could take tourists from port to port and guide them through all of your favorite adventures. That could work. Think big. Now think bigger!

Phil Capron

Now imagine where you could end up if you bought property worth $500,000. Like I said, this doesn't have to be done all in one purchase. it could be one, two, several, or dozens. Through one or several small decisions made early in your career, you can set yourself up to have close to half a million dollars.

Unless you're in a very high-priced market and you're a senior officer, it's unlikely you're going to hit this benchmark in one fell swoop. That's ok. A common misconception about the VA Loan is that you can only use it once. That is not true. We'll address this and other faulty folk lore surrounding this amazing benefit later. The important thing is that you see how your wealth creation goes up radically as these numbers grow.

Real Estate vs. the Stock Market

"PRESIDENT TRUMP AND I DON'T HAVE 401(K)S. THERE IS NO INSURANCE POLICY THAT WILL COVER A 401(K)" -ROBERT KIYOSAKI

Overall Returns

Trying to determine the comparison in returns between real estate and the stock market is like trying to find the truth about a particular event by watching coverage on Fox News and CNN about the same event. Depending on who is conducting the study or writing the news report, there is certainly an agenda. My agenda is educating you, the veteran, on the amazing benefit that is the VA Loan.

Numbers are skewed to fit an agenda by analyzing convenient timeframes (avoiding the dot com bubble for stocks, or the housing crisis of 2008), or spreading the study period out over such a long time period that major corrections in either market become statistically insignificant. If someone from the Air Force wants to really nerd out on this stuff and put it in a format that even a Marine can understand, I'll definitely include it in the second edition, but for now it's beyond the scope of this book to get too granular on this debate. For illustrative purposes, I'll concede that stocks do outperform real estate returns on average by a large margin. Let's use the following returns (on the rosy side for stocks, on the conservative side for real estate) as a benchmark for our discussion here.

Stocks: 9%

Real Estate: 3%

If the above is true, putting down this book and getting back to *Game of Thrones* would be a pretty good idea. I'm going to show you that it's not. Comparing stocks to residential real estate is like comparing apples to M-4s. We'll come back to the numbers above at the end of the chapter to do a final reconciliation. For now, let's look at the advantages of real estate that stocks do not enjoy.

Necessity

"I WILL FOREVER BELIEVE THAT BUYING A HOME IS A GREAT INVESTMENT. WHY? BECAUSE YOU CAN'T LIVE IN A STOCK CERTIFICATE." -OPRAH WINFREY

I recently attended a conference where Robert Helms of "The Real Estate Guys" radio show was the keynote speaker. The most powerful segment of his presentation to me, was the illustration that no human is ever, or will ever be, economically disconnected from real estate. Trends change, widgets come and go, technology is evolving at a breakneck pace. The one constant is that human beings, from caves to castles, from under bridges to 5th Avenue penthouses, will always need some place to live. Whether our currency is dollars or rubles, apples or M-4's, people will always pay to have a roof over their heads. With that in mind, currency doesn't matter, acquiring assets that are human necessities does.

Leverage:

"GIVE ME A LEVER LONG ENOUGH AND A FULCRUM ON WHICH TO PLACE IT, AND I SHALL MOVE THE WORLD"—ARCHIMEDES

Leverage may not move the world as Archimedes would have liked, but it certainly can move your bank account by a few zeros if you understand and apply this incredibly powerful principle. Here's a quick example:

Pick up the phone and give a stock broker a call. Let them you know you're interested in purchasing a large amount of (pick your favorite) stock. The broker should be quite eager to accept your money and make the acquisition, until they hear your terms. Tell them you'd like to buy $1,000,000 in stock, but you will only be bringing $200,000 and need them to arrange for someone else to pay off the remaining $800,000 over the next thirty years on your behalf. Oh, and you also expect to receive 100% of the dividends over the course of that time period.

If you actually did that, I suspect it didn't go well. Unless you are a sophisticated investor utilizing "put & call" options, you cannot utilize leverage in the stock market. The example above is precisely what happens when a person purchases a property the regular way using "conventional financing" which requires a 20% down payment. That individual is obtaining legal title and full enjoyment of the real property, and the bank has financed (you have leveraged) the remaining 80% of the purchase price.

From earlier in the chapter, you know how powerful it is to acquire even a small amount of real estate and start that snowball rolling downhill. Using the VA Loan, we're not leveraging 80%; we're leveraging up to 100% from the bank, guaranteed by the VA on our behalf!

Here is a quick example of leverage and why it can be so great in general. Let's use the example of the $100,000 house at a 5% interest rate and $400 per month in expenses in three different scenarios: a cash purchase, a conventional purchase with 20% down, and a VA Loan purchase with 0% down in order to compare the returns.

Type of Purchase	Mortgage Payment	Rent	Cashflow	Return on Investment
Cash	$0	$1,100	$700	8.4%

Conventional (20% Down)	$430	$1,100	$270	16.2%
VA (0% Down)	$536	$1,100	$164	Infinite Return

The example above illustrates the concept of "positive leverage" which basically means that the less that you have invested, the higher your return on a cash flowing property. The return and cash flow are inversely correlated, the "cash purchase" has the highest cash flow, but also the highest investment ($100,000). The VA Loan has the lowest cash flow ($164/mo.) but also has $0 invested making the return infinite.

Leverage is a powerful tool that should be used with care. The danger present with a highly leveraged position is its lack of cash flow. The cash purchase can afford to leave the property vacant a lot longer than the highly leveraged VA Loan; don't forget that when analyzing properties. Leverage is a double-edged sword, make sure you're not using it to give yourself a nasty, self-inflicted wound.

Higher Leverage = Higher Risk = Higher Returns

Imperfect Markets:

"REAL ESTATE CANNOT BE LOST OR STOLEN… MANAGED WITH REASONABLE CARE, IT IS ABOUT THE SAFEST INVESTMENT IN THE WORLD." -FRANKLIN D. ROOSEVELT

In the old days, stocks were traded in the "pits" at the New York Stock Exchange and others. You've probably seen the old pictures and videos of brokers yelling and screaming at each other and tallying trades on their little notebooks to be reconciled at the conclusion of the session. Obviously, everything is done by computer now and trades are executed with millisecond precision. At any time, you know precisely what the market value of a particular security is.

Back in the day, residential real estate was similarly unsophisticated. Prior to the Multiple Listing Service being available online and syndicated to third party websites where millions of potential homebuyers browse every year, brokers controlled the available listings in print books and faxed offers and counter offers back and forth to make deals. It might seem like both industries have evolved and the computer has leveled the playing field on both.

Looks can be deceiving, and I don't believe that is true.

Securities (stocks or bonds) are identical. They are traded apples to apples all day and every day the market is open. The market determines the value, period. Residential property is a completely different animal.

At the end of the day, it is a human on the other end of the transaction, not a series of inanimate trades catalogued by a computer in real time. As Robert Helms taught me, no human can ever be economically separated from the real estate market.

Humans are emotional creatures. The concept of home is perhaps one of the singular most emotional aspects of human existence. When engaging with a seller or a property, we need to conduct ourselves in a calm collected manner. Even though they may be selling "home," we are only buying a "house." Does that make sense?

Every piece of real estate is by definition, different. It is impossible for two homes to occupy the same exact piece of land. Neighborhoods are similar, home construction can be identical… but they are never absolutely the same. That's what makes real estate so special. We can employ superior market analysis, negotiation, patience, professional relationships, and instinct to create great real estate deals. The only reason we can do this is because we are operating in an imperfect market. And that's why I love real estate! Every day I get to hunt for the opportunity to create a deal with my expertise, not buy and hope the CEO's and boards of the stocks I purchase are looking out for me as much as they're looking out for themselves. At the time of printing, the company "We Work" is going through a very public and very catastrophic collapse. I'm sure glad I invested in myself instead of them!

Forced Appreciation/Control

"Every person who invests in well-selected real estate in a growing section of a prosperous community adopts the surest and safest method of becoming independent, for real estate is the basis of wealth." -Theodore Roosevelt

Leverage is great, and is certainly one of the main reasons I love real estate. The control or influence of outcome through strategic acquisition, management, and disposition as well as the ability to force appreciation, are a couple of other reasons.

What is "Forced Appreciation?" Simply put, it is an owner's ability to increase the value of a piece of property by improving the property physically, making it produce more revenue through superior management, or possibly changing the use of the property to a higher and better one (adding a bedroom, Airbnb, changing the zoning, et cetera).

When investing in a public company, I have no control over the board, the CEO, or competitors that could unseat my seemingly wise investment. My money is a leaf in the wind. It was blowing the right way when I bought it, but who knows which way it will turn over the course of my ownership?

With a piece of real property, I know exactly where it sits within the submarket when I buy it. I buy it with built in "equity" right off the bat by utilizing the concept of the imperfect market and taking advantage of the opportunity to negotiate human to human—not in a malicious or underhanded way, but by simply advocating for my interests in a straightforward and honest fashion. Once the property is mine, I can select the right manager to act on my behalf and monitor them to ensure they are acting in my best interest. I can select great tenants who I suspect will stick around for a while and who I believe will take great care of my property. I can select the most opportune time to refinance or dispose of the property for maximum gain. I can use the property as a tax shelter and employ legal methods to defer taxes. These are control levers that simply don't exist in the stock trading world.

Forced Appreciation is the most powerful force that has propelled me from newly separated and beaten down in 2012, to financially free and happier than ever in 2019. I love all of the ways that real estate conspires to grow my wealth every minute, of every hour, of every day, no matter what it is that I choose to do during that time.

This book is about your VA Loan, which was my gateway into a different world. It was the red pill that enabled me to completely transform the way I view money and work. So, let's talk about that for a little bit, shall we?

Chapter Four:

The VA Loan

The VA Loan is the Cadillac of residential loan products. Created immediately after World War 2 concluded, the intent was to help veterans returning from Europe and the Pacific reacclimate to civilian life by offering them a slice of the American Dream, home ownership.

Under this program, the Department of Veterans Affairs (VA) promises lending institutions that if they offer a home loan to veterans, it will be guaranteed by the US government in the unlikely event of a default (failure of the veteran to pay). Because of this government guarantee, banks tend to offer lower rates on VA Loans than other competitive loan products. Here are the top advantages of utilizing a VA Loan:

- No down payment required
- Lower interest rates
- No private mortgage insurance requirement
- Relatively easy loan application process

No Down Payment Required

Other loan programs, like conventional loans and Federal Housing Administration (FHA) loans require down payments. Conventional loans are often 20% of the purchase price, and FHA loans are at least 3.5% of the purchase price. For a young service member, 3.5% can represent an insurmountable hurdle based on their income. On a modest $200,000 house, that's a $7,000 down payment at best with an FHA Loan (3.5% down) or a staggering $40,000 down with a conventional product (20% down). The VA Loan enables America's best to achieve home ownership with 0% down, opening the door to purchasing a home to more veterans than would otherwise be able to achieve that goal.

Lower Interest Rates

As much as I wish the banks offering loans to veterans through the VA Loan program cut rates to say "thank you for your service," it's simply not the case. They are large corporations who are accountable to their shareholders, so that is not their motivation for offering lower rates to veterans. The banks offer lower rates on VA Loans because the government, through the Department of Veterans Affairs, promises payment on behalf of the veteran. If a veteran fails to pay their loan, the VA will intercede before the bank forecloses (takes the property back from the homeowner) and attempt to help the veteran get the loan current. If that fails, the VA will often foreclose on the property instead of the bank.

Since the VA is guaranteeing the payment, they pay the bank what they are owed, then attempt to resell the asset to recoup some of their losses. This government guarantee to the banks is very powerful, and it grants VA Loan buyers a massive advantage in the next section: private mortgage insurance.

Private Mortgage Insurance (PMI)

Private Mortgage Insurance is what the Conventional Loans and FHA Loans require to give the lending institution the same warm and fuzzy they get with the VA Loan, which as previously mentioned, features a government guarantee. However, instead of a government guarantee, the cost of Private Mortgage Insurance is passed on to the buyer.

There are several variables when calculating PMI, but for a quick illustration, let's use an example of $100 per month on the same $200,000 house from above. Using the FHA Loan, we are now not only paying $7,000 as a down payment versus $0 with a VA Loan, but we would be on the hook for an additional $100 per month in PMI.

The VA Loan truly is the Cadillac of residential mortgages, and the lack of a PMI requirement has a lot to do with that fact.

Relatively Easy Application and Underwriting

As mentioned earlier, the VA guarantee gives the banks great flexibility and the incentive to lend to veterans. With that in mind, there actually is no minimum credit score required to obtain a VA Loan. If a qualifying veteran borrower passes the lending institution's criteria, the VA will support the loan.

Lenders also tend to have more lenient standards with their "Debt to Income Ratio," which is the amount you owe versus the amount you make every month. Applying for any type of loan can be frustrating, but the VA makes the process relatively painless by taking care of a lot of the eligibility documentation on behalf of the borrower through the lender. They will still need your LES (if you're active duty), 2 years' tax returns, bank statements, and the ability to pull your credit. For a complete list of requirements to apply for a VA Loan, go to:

www.yourvaloanandhowitcanmakeyouamillionaire.com

Who is Eligible for a VA Loan?

Eligibility has different benchmarks based on when you served, but it is quite lenient as a whole. As little as ninety days of active duty service post 9/11 qualifies. A lender will determine whether you are eligible for a VA Loan by requesting what is called a "Certificate of Eligibility" directly from the VA on your behalf.

In addition to service requirements, you should also strive to obtain the highest possible credit score, which will help you obtain the lowest possible rate, and make sure to have stable income. I learned the hard way when I left active duty that income verification is very important to the lender when the purchase of a duplex, I had under contract for a great price fell through when the lender discovered I was separating from active duty.

We could spend ten pages outlining every scenario of qualification or denial, but the focus of this book is to show you how to use optimal strategy in the utilization of your VA loan, not putting you to sleep reading a bunch of lending regulations. Later, we will talk about your VA Loan Team. A great mortgage lender will help you navigate this step with no problem.

Unfortunately, there is a lot of misinformation floating around regarding the VA Loan. Let's take a look at some of the most common:

VA Loan Myths

If you don't use it, you lose it

Just because you didn't use your VA Loan eligibility on active duty, doesn't mean you've forfeited it. As noted above, approval is relatively easy compared to other loan types. The lender you choose will help you apply for your Certificate of Eligibility directly through the Department of Veteran's Affairs website.

You can only use your VA Loan once, make it count!

That's simply not true. You can actually have two VA Loans at the same time through "second tier eligibility." Even after you've used your second-tier eligibility, you can sell or refinance and recapture your initial eligibility once again. A great strategy we'll talk about later in the book is to accumulate enough equity in a property purchased using a VA Loan to refinance with a Conventional Loan that does not require PMI.

Usually, the amount of equity (difference between what is owed on the loan and the property's value) is 20%. Utilizing this strategy, you can leapfrog into additional properties at 0% down over the course of your military career. Utilizing this strategy, it is certainly possible to acquire over $1,000,000 in property using your VA Loan multiple times over the course of your career.

You can use your VA Loan for investment property

This is a dangerous myth that can really get a service member in trouble if they go through with a purchase as an investment. In order to purchase a property using a VA Loan, you must sign a certification stating that you intend to occupy the property as your primary residence.

I've heard of people who have closed on properties with no intention to occupy them, scamming the system, and putting the rest of us at risk. Not only is that a mark on your honor, but it's also a little thing called "loan fraud," which is kind of a big deal. Do not, I repeat, DO NOT listen to someone advising you to lie and defraud the government. It's simply not worth it.

The VA Loan is an amazing benefit to all of us as written, there's no reason to cheat. Be investment minded when you purchase the property, but understand you will be living there for a time to be compliant with the terms of your loan.

You can't buy an expensive property with a VA Loan

Congress is in the midst of changing the maximum loan amount, which if approved, will take effect in 2020. Prior to this change, most counties had a maximum VA Loan amount around $450,000.

This myth is incorrect. Even under the old rule, you could purchase a more expensive property using a VA Loan; however, you would be responsible for a down payment of 25% of the difference between the maximum entitlement for your area and the purchase price. For example, if the max allowable loan amount in your county was $450,000, and you purchased a home for

$550,000, the VA would still guarantee the loan just like any other property so long as you paid $25,000 as a down payment.

In this hypothetical purchase, your 4.5% down payment would still eliminate the need for Private Mortgage Insurance and get you the house you want, so it's still a good deal for most borrowers. I suspect there will be continued changes to loan limits under the VA program after this writing. For the latest information, go to:

www.yourvaloanandhowitcanmakeyouamillionaire.com

The VA rips off veterans with the "Funding Fee"

The VA Funding Fee is a charge that can be rolled into your loan and is the cost of accessing this amazing loan product. It is usually not money out of your pocket, but it is money you are borrowing, so it does cost you. The first time VA Loan Funding Fee is 2.15% and it varies from borrower to borrower. Subsequent uses result in a slightly higher funding fee. Consult your lender for exact terms based on your situation.

Because this funding fee enables me to acquire primary residences at 0% with no Private Mortgage Insurance, I will happily pay it every day and twice on Sunday! I rely on my ability to select the right property with built in equity and high potential for future upside through rent growth and appreciation to offset this relatively small fee. The VA uses these fees to fund their operation and enable more veterans to obtain home loans through the program. If you have a service-connected disability rating, your funding fee may be waived.

Qualification for a VA Loan is difficult

More veterans than ever are taking advantage of the VA Loan. The number of loans the Department of Veterans Affairs has been rising steadily since the early 2000s, and over twenty million home loans have been issued since World War 2.

Dealing with any lender can be a bit of a process; but in general, lenders are more flexible with VA Loans than any other residential mortgage product. If you don't qualify for a VA Loan due to credit, debt, or income issues, it's unlikely you will qualify for an FHA or Conventional loan either. Get to the bottom of your financial issues as quickly as possible so you are eligible for the best possible interest rate on your purchase.

The VA might cause the purchase contract to fall through

Yes, the Department of Veterans Affairs is a government agency. The jokes write themselves.

If you've been to a VA Medical Center you know the bureaucracy is nauseating, even if you felt fine entering the hospital. In my experience, the folks working there are true professionals and want the best for veterans; it's the bureaucracy that makes it a sometimes-painful experience. The good news? The VA doesn't have a whole lot of input once you've found your property and obtained a contract to purchase.

Your lender would have already secured your Certificate of Eligibility to ensure you qualify for a VA Loan, so the only thing left in their purview is the VA Appraisal. Because the VA is guaranteeing your loan, they need to make sure the property is in good condition and that the amount you're borrowing reflects a fair market value for the property.

I've seen people get in trouble because of the property condition during my career in real estate. If the property has obvious safety hazards or deficiencies, the appraiser will notate them and instruct that they be fixed prior to closing.

Sometimes, the seller refuses to do the repairs, and that's the source of the problem. A way to avoid this potential snag is to lean on the experience of your real estate agent, the keystone of your VA Loan Team, and get ahead of any condition items that might make the appraiser raise an eyebrow. For more information on the kinds of things the VA appraiser looks for go to www.yourvaloanandhowitcanmakeyouamillionaire.com.

It's unbelievable how much misinformation there is going around about the VA Loan, and even more amazing how many active duty service members and veterans don't understand that the program truly is available to them. This book is my attempt to help fix that. If you're finding value here, don't keep it a secret! Tell your buddies at the command or on Facebook. We want as many of our brothers and sisters to have a piece of the American Dream and to have the ability to work towards financial freedom, using the VA Loan as a stepping stone.

I hope by now you're a believer in real estate as the most understandable, attainable, financeable, controllable, and widely accessible investment asset class that there is in this world. The VA Loan opens the door to almost everybody who has honorably served to get a jump start, ideally with zero money down.

So, how do you actually use your VA Loan? Here's a quick step-by-step process to get you familiar with the process.

VA Loan: 9 Line

1. Make a Decision: Is Buying Right for You?

"It is in your moments of decision that your destiny is shaped" - Tony Robbins

There are several critical factors when considering whether homebuying is a good option for you at the current time. A recurring theme in this book is that you have to stretch your comfort zone in order to have the best that life has to offer. Ultimately, that requires a decision. Is the juice worth the squeeze?

I'm sure you've experienced this quandary many times thus far in your life. The decision to purchase a home is no different. The road less traveled requires courage to set foot upon, but since you're reading this book, I know that courage is not the issue. You need to take a hard look at your options, weigh the pros and cons, and make the best decision for your situation. For many, it is easy to accept a voucher for a place on base, eliminating the need to worry about maintenance or mortgages. The price of convenience is steep, however.

Let's take a look at an example of an E-5 who has just been given authorization to leave the barracks to apply for base housing, rent an apartment, or purchase a home of their own. The E-5 has a Basic Allowance for Housing entitlement of $1,200 per month and is torn between hitting the easy button and staying on base, trying a little harder to find a rental for themselves or to share with a roommate, or to finally purchase a home of their own, either solo or with one roommate.

Housing Type/ Money	Base	Apartment: Solo	Apartment with Roommate	Your House	Your House with Roommate
Basic Allowance for Housing	$0	$1,200/mo.	$1,200/mo.	$1,200/mo.	$1,200/mo.
Rent or Mortgage	$0	$1,000	$500	$1,000	$500
CASH FLOW	$0	$200	$700	$200	$700
Net worth increases due to amortization and appreciation over 5 years	$0	$0	$0	$63,765	$63,765

Plus, Cash flow over 5 years	$0	$0	$0	$12,000	$42,000
Total	$0	$0	$0	$75,765	$105,765

There are many variables involved in calculating the rent versus buy analysis for your particular situation, but in almost every instance, buying and ideally leveraging a renter (roommate) is going to outperform your other options by a wide margin. If our example was your reality, what would you do with an extra $100,000 five years from now?

It is clear that owning property is a superior decision financially, next we have to determine if it makes sense for our lifestyle. Are you single or married? Do you have kids? Are you comfortable living with others or do you require the respite of living alone after long days and stressors at work? If you're still on active duty, how long are your orders at your current duty station? Will you have the option to extend or select new orders at the same station? Are you approaching the end of your service career? If so, would you like to stay in the house you buy after separation or retirement? Are there good job prospects for you in that market?

These questions as well as countless others are driven by your circumstances. They are important to consider as you decide whether purchasing a home is right for you at this time. If you believe in the power of real estate as a vehicle to achieve financial freedom, you'll need to take a hard look at your finances to make sure it's a smart play based on your situation.

As you will see in subsequent chapters, your credit can have a huge impact on the purchase you're about to make. Banks offer their best rates to the most qualified applicants. They may still offer you a loan with credit blemishes and other budget factors that can be corrected relatively easily, but the difference in monthly payment can be profound and negatively affect your long-term plans. This is not the sexiest step of the process, but it is critically important to your success.

As you know, the VA Loan is available to qualified active duty service members and veterans with no down payment required. However, embarking on a home buying adventure without your financial ducks in a row is a mistake. When I worked as a residential real estate agent, it would make me cringe when offers would come in on my listings with a $500 "earnest money deposit" (a refundable deposit a buyer makes to show the seller they are a "serious" buyer and to comply with contract law) and my seller would "counter offer" with a higher amount like $1,000 and the other agent would inform me that their VA buyer "didn't have it."

Yes, you read that correctly…

There are people out there using their VA Loans with $500 to their name. It's like putting tomatoes in a fruit salad. Just because you can, doesn't mean that you should. The most heart wrenching stories of VA Loan failures stemmed from individuals purchasing homes who really shouldn't have, and then collapsing under the weight of a fairly normal life event. A few examples are ending their active duty career, paying for a significant home repair, or relocating and failing to pay the mortgage while their property manager was looking for a new tenant.

Just because you can purchase a property with 0% down, does not mean that you don't need money. Life happens. A savings account specifically for your property or access to at least six months' worth of expenses is a great place to start when purchasing property, especially your first one! If you've decided that buying a home is best for your circumstances, prepare to dig deeper into financials in step 2!

2. Ask Your Bank for a Pre-Approval

When deciding which item to list as step #2, I faced a Coke versus Pepsi type debate amongst my colleagues in the real estate industry. Who should a buyer call first? The real estate agent (Coke), or the mortgage lender (Pepsi)? After much deliberation, it is my belief you should approach a lender first.

Many homebuyers start calling real estate agents or worse; clicking around on a real estate website ensuring they'll receive calls from dozens of agents and lenders about properties they don't even remember looking at, when they don't even know if they have the ability to purchase a home. In step #1 we made a decision and took a look at our cash in the bank and perhaps glanced at our credit report, but the bank or mortgage broker who will assist you with obtaining your VA Loan will require much more.

The reason I recommend requesting a pre-approval with your bank is because they already have a relationship with you. They will have some of your data from accounts, direct deposit, car loans, credit cards, and so forth. With this information and authorization to perform an inquiry on your credit, they will be able to make a fairly accurate determination about what you will qualify for a home purchase. This process is called "pre-approval" and all home sellers and real estate agents representing them will want to see this document as a part of your offer to purchase.

Formal loan application is not the most pleasant task, as they'll need everything short of a blood sample to comply with regulations and get your loan approved. However, at this stage, we're just trying to get a ballpark of where you stand financially, what you can afford, and how that fits within your plan for life at this stage. If there are issues with your credit, income, tax returns, or anything else about your financial position, it is best to know now before you go house hunting. I have seen several people fall in love with homes only to find out they can't qualify to purchase them and it's not fun.

Let's make sure it doesn't happen to you by contacting your bank before you go shopping!

3. Select a Real Estate Agent/ Buyer's Consult

If you start browsing homes online prior to interviewing real estate agents, beware! The big online sites only have one goal, which is to capture your information and sell it to real estate agents and mortgage lenders. I've heard of agents paying hundreds of dollars just for one person's information; it's big business! Keep that in mind when you are clicking around and feel tempted to submit your information in exchange for a little more information about a property. The site will likely make you register for an account with them to view all listings, photos, and information—which is fine; just don't click on "request more information" or any of the similar calls to action. If you do, you'll be receiving more calls from virtual assistants in other countries, agents, and lenders than you know what to do with.

You'll welcome the spammers calling from the "Social Security Administration" about a "fraudulent use of your Social Security Number" just to break up the monotony of real estate call after real estate call. If you do click for more information in a moment of weakness to get more information about your dream house, you'll find that the vast majority of the time, it's not the listing agent (the one who is representing the seller) who calls. Your information has been sold to someone else who knows no more about the property than you do. You need a true professional in your corner, somebody who understands your goals and needs. Your real estate agent is your #1 ally, so it's important to pick the right one.

Markets ebb and flow from a "buyer's" to a "neutral" to a "seller's" market. To the unindoctrinated, buying or selling a house can seem like a fairly static act. When I was selling real estate, it would kill me when a buyer would tell me "back when I bought my last house, we did it THIS way" which usually flew in the face of my professional advice. I'd inquire as to exactly when the last house was purchased… 1983.

"Sir, unfortunately I can't comment on that market, as I was not alive at that time."

You need somebody who understands the local market, customs, and can "read the tea leaves" to give you the best possible advice for what will be the largest purchase of your life to this point. We will dive deep into what makes a great real estate agent in a future chapter. Right now, you just need to understand how important your real estate agent is, and what to expect during your buyer's consult.

The "Buyer's Consult" is usually your first meeting with your agent, and will take place in their office. A great way to know if you're interviewing a successful agent is that they ask for your "pre-approval" prior to meeting with you. Agents only get paid when they help their clients buy or sell a home, the best agents can't afford to spend their valuable time with those who are not approved to purchase a property. Once they know you are pre-approved for a VA Loan, they will invite you in to meet at their office.

During this meeting, they should get to know you and your needs and wants. They should ask great questions to help you dial in on your criteria for a house. They will educate you on current market conditions based on their experience. After they have a good idea of what you're looking for, they will show you what's currently available on the market and set up an automatic search through the local Multiple Listing Service (MLS) that alerts both of you when a matching property hits the market. After your automatic search is live, you will begin to receive new properties via email periodically. When these emails arrive, look at them promptly and respond to your agent immediately if you'd like to set up a tour. As the old saying goes "if you sleep on it, you might not sleep in it!"

4. Shop Lenders

But Phil, we got pre-approved at step 1 with our bank! Why are we revisiting lenders?

I know. Hear me out please…

The wrong real estate agent can cost you money by getting you into a bad deal. By not understanding market value and trends, by failing as a negotiator, or by not sending it to you in a timely fashion, they could even cost you the house of your dreams.

The lender can cost you even more money than the agent, and they can make you lose your dream house, too. People spend the most time searching for the perfect house and negotiating a contract, slightly less vetting their real estate agent, and way less evaluating their loan options. This is a mistake I want to help you avoid!

Our country was built on—and continues to thrive on—the principles of capitalism. Competition in business is a good thing for innovation and for the consumer! Just the act of alerting a bank or mortgage broker that you are interviewing others and reviewing their proposals as well will incentivize them to give you their best offer in an attempt to win your business. Just like the real estate agent, the lender only gets paid when a loan closes (when you buy a home, the lender sends the money to the attorney for closing, and you start making your mortgage payments as agreed). The lender and agent both really want your purchase to be successful as it's in their interest to do so. As a consumer, we need to know enough about how both of their businesses operate to make sure we are getting the best possible service from both.

5. Tour Properties

Finally! Am I right? It's step FIVE and we're FINALLY going to look at a house! Woohoo!

You've been reviewing automatic emails from your real estate agent and inquired about the best-looking options, and now it's time to set foot inside. I'm sure you're excited to finally tour a property; but think about it, what have we invested in this process so far? Ten hours? Maybe?

I know guys that spend way more time than that deliberating over their next car, truck, or bike. Relax. This purchase is going to be the largest of your life to this point. I implore you to give it the respect it deserves. Because you've been monitoring the market through your agent's emails, you should have a feel for what is happening in your preferred neighborhoods, an understanding of whether the market favors buyers or sellers, and ideally you have a pretty good idea of what criteria are most important to you. It may take one tour, or it may take several; it may take dozens, but eventually, you will find "the one" and write an offer.

6. Negotiate Contract

Once you've found "the one" you should submit an offer through your real estate agent as quickly as possible. Timing is highly market dependent, but action always beats inaction.

Since you've determined that this is your best option, you want to move with a purpose. Lean on your agent to obtain more information through the Listing Agent (the agent representing the seller). You'll want to know:

- if there are other offers or potential offers in play,
- how long the property has been on the market,
- if there is any flexibility on price,
- why the seller is selling,
- if they are willing to do any repairs or give a credit for unsatisfactory condition items,
- if they are willing to contribute to buyer's closing costs,
- and many other questions.

A great agent is worth their weight in gold during this phase of the process. Tens of thousands of dollars can be won or lost at this point, and that compounds into truly massive sums of money over the course of your ownership of the property. The primary terms outlined in a purchase contract are as follows:

- Price
- Earnest Money Deposit
- Financing (VA Loan)
- Inspection Contingency
- Appraisal Contingency
- Closing Date

7. Due Diligence

Unless you are a very sophisticated buyer—which I assume you are not, as you're reading this section of the book—I do not recommend writing a contract "non-contingent" or "as-is." Your contingency period (usually around a week) allows you to inspect the property with a professional, review any state mandated disclosures, review any homeowner's association or condominium documents, obtain insurance quotes, and evaluate a number of other market specific items. This is your time to make sure the property is everything you believe it is. Do not take this lightly; use it wisely!

There are three aspects to your due diligence period which are:

- Physical Due Diligence

- Financial Due Diligence

- Neighborhood Due Diligence

Physical Due Diligence

Your real estate agent is a great resource and should be able to spot major physical problems during your initial property tour. But once you're under contract to purchase a property, it is critical to hire a professional home inspector.

A great home inspector will be able to educate you on condition concerns throughout the property and provide you with a comprehensive report of their findings. It is important to understand the difference between cosmetic items and issues that affect the structure, function, or safety of the building.

In addition to an overall condition report, an inspection for termites, moisture, lead, asbestos, radon, and other area-specific concerns will be conducted at this time. Your real estate agent will know which studies are applicable based on the property location and any additional reports your lender requires. After you have had time to review the reports with your agent and inspector, you may renegotiate the terms of the contract in the event there is a legitimate concern with the property.

As in the previous negotiation phase, your real estate agent is indispensable during this phase. His or her function at this stage is to make the case for any items you are requesting and to do so in a way that will not offend the seller and blow the deal up.

The home inspector will give you a very detailed report, and weak buyer's agents sometimes mistakenly send the entire list for the seller to address. This is a sure-fire way to blow up a deal. You should only request items that are deal breakers for you and are hazards to the structure, safety, or major systems of the property.

Financial Due Diligence

The VA will send an appraiser to verify the purchase reflects current market value for the property, but there are additional steps you can take to ensure you're making a wise financial decision. You will need help from two members of your team: your real estate agent and your property manager. Both will perform a CMA, or "comparative market analysis" for you. The real estate agent will base their analysis on other homes that have recently sold and others that are currently listed for sale.

The property manager will base their analysis on similar homes that have recently rented and others that are currently listed for rent. You can help both of your team members by looking at the big real estate sites for publicly available information on both sales and rentals, but the real estate agent and property manager will have access to even more data to help you make the best possible decision.

Market conditions vary widely, but we always strive to acquire properties at a discount, or "with equity" when we purchase them. It's also a good idea to purchase a property that will rent for more than your mortgage payment and reasonable expenses the day you purchase it. Whether you stay in the property for many years or need to rent or sell due to a military transfer or other life circumstances soon after purchase, it sure is nice to have multiple options at that time.

In addition to taking steps to ensure you are truly buying well from a market value and market rent perspective, this is also your opportunity to double check expense assumptions. Insurance quotes can vary based on a number of factors. Make sure to obtain a quote from your preferred insurance company as well as one or two others to shop pricing and coverage. In certain markets, additional coverage could be required for flood or tornado damage. Make sure you have all lender required coverage quoted as well as any other "insurance riders" that may be applicable to the property in question.

Another big expense is property tax. Find out what the change in assessment will be during this inspection period and make sure it's within your comfort range. Every locality is different in how they calculate changing tax rates. These additional costs could be a deal breaker if discovered during due diligence. If you fail to obtain accurate quotes during due diligence and find out later, it will be too late and at best, you'll lose your earnest money deposit for failing to close on the property. At worst, the seller could file a lawsuit for breach of contract!

Neighborhood Due Diligence

The best house in a declining, stigmatized, or troubled neighborhood will lose value over time, instead of appreciating. While the macro economy depends on global and national level policy and events, real estate markets are local and even hyper local. Where you buy matters! As the old saying goes, "location, location, and location!"

There are a couple key areas of neighborhood due diligence that your real estate may not be able to assist you with, by law. Certain provisions of various "fair housing" laws prohibit real estate agents from answering questions or providing information about the neighborhood in question. The laws were instituted to make sure all people have equal access to housing, and potential buyers aren't being "steered" to or from particular neighborhoods. The unintended consequence of the legislation is the muzzling of real estate agents from providing their clients the best possible information. (Good thing I'm not a real estate agent!)

Here are the key issues of concern that your real estate agent might not be able to give you a straight answer on:

Crime—If your physical security isn't reason enough to select a home away from high crime areas, think about your financial security. Most people prefer not to live in high crime areas if they have the choice. Here is a good online resource to search your neighborhood and the area immediately surrounding the home you have under contract:

www.communitycrimemap.com

Schools—Even if you don't have children, many prospective buyers and renters are searching around schools of a particular rating. It is a good idea to incorporate schools into your initial neighborhood search criteria. Even if they aren't applicable to you directly, it's helpful to understand where different schools and school districts in your market rank. Just like the actual home, renters and buyers with children will gravitate towards the best possible schools available to them. Here is a good resource to compare schools in your search:

www.greatschools.org

It took great courage to submit your first offer and sign a purchase agreement with the seller. Now that you've had a chance to review all of the due diligence information you've collected utilizing the team members and resources listed above and can make an educated decision on whether you should proceed with the contract, renegotiate, or release. This can be an even more stressful part of the process than the initial negotiation! If information is discovered that makes this property untenable, don't be afraid to go back to the drawing board and find a property that meets your needs. If you still want to proceed with the contract, let's see what else is required to get it to the finish line.

8. Contract to Close

Assuming everything is satisfactory during your inspections, at this time, you will "remove contingencies" and proceed to closing. At this stage, your agent is helping direct traffic between your lender and your closing company or attorney, as well as keeping you and the seller's agent updated on the progress of the transaction.

The lender will order an appraisal to ensure they are deploying their capital wisely in your new home, and that it is in fact "worth" the purchase price—or, if you're following the guidelines found in this book, ideally the appraisal comes in higher, so you close on the house with built-in equity. Equity doesn't put money in your pocket at this point, but it does wonders to pad the ego and make you sleep well at night.

It is important that during the entire home buying process, you not do anything that will impact your credit, your employment, or your bank accounts. You submitted a bunch of information to the lender for your pre-approval and since, but now that the loan is heading towards closing, the lender will want to verify all of the information that they have on file and ensure you are still a qualified buyer.

Want to buy a new car, all the furniture for the new house, and quit your job? Fantastic! Just please wait until after closing to do so. I've seen deals blow up for those three reasons and others between inspections and closing, because the buyer damaged some portion of their credit profile with the lender and knocked themselves out of loan qualification.

Your attorney or title company will be working in the background with your lender and with the seller's attorney to ensure a smooth closing. They need to make sure any open mortgages the seller has on the property can be paid at closing. They will also do a search to make sure the seller doesn't have any judgements or pending litigation against them that could attach to the property and cause you problems after closing.

Your attorney will also prepare the documents to record that you are now the new owner with the municipality. With the title search satisfactorily completed and an appraisal at or above your purchase price, you will be counting the days until closing!

9. Closing Day!

Hooray! You've made it! Just kidding, the journey has just begun.

After you sign the mountain of lender required documents pledging all but your first born and your soul to the satisfaction of the debt you're incurring, and the attorney documents making everything legal eagle, you'll receive your keys and be a homeowner. Congrats!

Before closing, make sure to do a thorough "final walk through" of the property with your real estate agent. The purpose of this last visit before signing paperwork is to ensure nothing has materially changed since you last saw it (think falling trees, burst water heater, fire, HVAC system failing, et cetera. I've seen them all). It's also an opportunity to ensure any repairs the seller had agreed to make as part of your "property inspection contingency removal" have been completed.

This may come as a surprise to you, but the lender and both buyer and seller's attorneys are quite busy in the days leading up to closing. There is a lot of back and forth to make sure the seller's loan (if applicable) is being paid off, as well as their share of taxes and other fees called "pro rations" and that you as the buyer are picking up on the day of closing.

Often, there are invoices for repair work completed by third party contractors that are paid at closing. Perhaps your agent negotiated a home warranty to be included with your purchase (always a good idea!) and let's not forget about the real estate agents' commissions—they have worked hard to get you into your new home. With all of this correspondence involving multiple parties, it is a fairly common occurrence for something to fall through the cracks and closing to be delayed. I've done this dance dozens of times personally and with clients. My advice to you is to have some flexibility with your closing date.

Some of the most chaotic experiences I've had in real estate have occurred when the buyer's moving truck was sitting outside of their new home, but for whatever reason, the property had failed to close on time. He who is most flexible, wins! Do everything in your power to give yourself that flexibility, just in case.

In the SWCC Teams, every man on the boat had a particular job—or usually, several. My jobs were Comms, Nav, manning the .50 cal. mounted on the bow, and monitoring the FLIR when necessary. My counterpart on the other side of the coxswain was in charge of our weapons, monitoring the gauges, and being prepared to make any repairs to the craft if needed, as well as manning the M240 located on the stern. If I had a problem with my .50, I wouldn't be calling him to come up from the stern, I'd just fix it. If something happens to me, he'd know the chart and waypoints well enough to get us out of harm's way, and how to call in a nine line for me.

Your real estate team should operate in a similar manner. The only difference is that no matter what your rank, you're the OIC for this mission. You won't know the intricacies of loan processing to the same level as your mortgage officer, nor should you. Your real estate agent will definitely be better at running the Comparable Market Analysis—as they should be. However, you are the boss and you need to have an understanding of the roles and responsibilities for all of your team members and oversee their performance.

Chapter Five:

Your VA Loan Team

Since you've read this far, you are ready to build your team of professionals who will be invaluable to you in your search and acquisition. I've seen folks make a mess of real estate transactions by thinking they were smarter than the professionals who do this every day for a living.

Your Real Estate Agent

Your real estate agent is the most important member of your team. If you're the OIC, they are your Chief or First Sergeant. They will help you navigate unfamiliar waters, avoid storms and shoals, and get to your destination with your treasure intact. The best part of using a real estate agent as a buyer? The seller pays them, not you.

That's right, when a homeowner lists their home for sale with a real estate broker, they actually decide what they will offer the "buyer's broker" in exchange for bringing them (the seller) a qualified, willing, and able buyer for the purchase of their property. The other great part of utilizing a buyer's broker is that once entering into an agency agreement with them (signing a document agreeing to work together), they are obligated to look out for your financial interests. This is also known as acting as your "fiduciary." Since it doesn't cost you anything, using a buyer's agent is a no-brainer. You will be entrusting this agent, your fiduciary, with the largest purchase of your life to this point, so it's important to take care in selecting the right one.

Believe it or not, most states require more hours of training for a new hair stylist than a new real estate agent. We're all veterans, so we know the horrors of a bad haircut... but the consequences of a bad real estate purchase are worse than even the gnarliest high and tight. Here are a few questions you can ask to make sure you are dealing with a professional, and not just someone who has passed the state required training and tests.

- How long have you been in real estate?
- How many transactions did you complete in the past year?
- What areas do you serve?
- How many VA Loan transactions have you completed in your career?
- Can you give me an example of a transaction in which you negotiated a great deal for your client?
- Are you willing to provide CMAs prior to writing an offer in order to make sure my offer is representative of fair market value (or hopefully, less than market value)?
- What steps do you take to ensure there are no problems with the VA appraiser with the property's condition and value?
- How many clients are you working with currently? Will you have time to show me properties when they become available?
- Do you have an assistant or other team members?
- May I contact several of your past clients?

You can use these ideas to come up with a list tailor made to your specific needs. Don't forget, your real estate agent is working for you. Setting expectations up front is critical to a successful business relationship. Referrals are a great way to obtain a few prospective real estate agents. Be sure to only accept referrals from someone who has used that particular real estate agent in a transaction. Just because someone is your friend, your friend's wife, or otherwise connected to your social circle, does not make them the best agent for you. If I were looking for an agent, here are a few things that would be on my radar.

I would look for a professional that has been in the business for several years, is actively practicing real estate as their only job (no part timers), is closing at least ten transactions per year (to stay current on market trends, procedure, and negotiation), and ultimately someone who I believe has my best interest at heart. I would acknowledge that the agent will only get paid upon a successful closing, and remind myself of this fact during negotiations with the seller to make sure the agent is still acting in my best interest and according to my wishes.

I would search for an agent who has some experience working with investors, because I do not wish to pay market value for a property. I would make sure they responded to my requests to tour properties or for more information in a timely fashion, and that we communicate and work well together. Ultimately, you will decide which aspects of an agent's professional resume are most important to you and who will best represent your interests, but those items would be at the top of my list if I were using my VA Loan again today.

Using the criteria you establish at your "buyer's consultation," your agent will guide you through the best available homes in your area. They will work closely with the listing agent to obtain all of the information about the properties that interest you, and they will also give you their professional opinion on the home's value and any negotiation points that can be used in your favor. They should know what the VA appraiser is looking for regarding property condition and will be able to spot landmines you might miss, saving you time, money, and heartache. Your real estate agent truly is the most valuable member of your team, so take care to select the right one for you. If you need additional assistance finding a great agent, drop us a line at:

www.yourvaloanandhowitcanmakeyouamillionaire.com

Should I Become a Real Estate Agent?

I'm stealing my attorney's favorite answer: "It depends."

As you know from Chapter 1, I was a real estate agent for several years. It was a great experience for me, and I certainly wouldn't be where I am today if I didn't obtain my license. Without it, I would have never known about the problems surrounding the VA Loan and would not have endeavored to write this book.

I loved helping my friends and teammates buy their first houses and tried to get them to understand the concepts in this book long before I'd taken the time to write them down. It taught me how to analyze a market, understand what the appraiser was looking for, and gave me first-hand experience in hundreds of high stakes negotiations. Being a real estate agent was great for me, but if you remember... I didn't have many options when I separated from service unexpectedly.

It took almost six months to get my first commission check, and it was for peanuts. I had to triage bills and live lean for those early months until I was established. It's a great career for some people, but the overwhelming majority of people who hold real estate licenses don't actually sell any houses! Most don't survive their first year as a licensed agent, and quit. It's a hard way to make an easy living!

So, for most people, I don't believe it's going to be the right fit... but you will have to make that decision for yourself. The barrier to entry to become a real estate agent is quite low, in many states a forty-hour course and a "C" on the state and national exams is good enough. Here are a few pros and cons of becoming licensed yourself:

Pros:

- Access to the "multiple listing service" where you can see more detailed information about each listing not shared on the public websites, access tax information, in some states see what the property sold for previously, and what type of loan the seller has, if applicable;

- The ability to access properties on your time, without having to coordinate with a buyer's agent;

- Making a commission on the purchase of your house or applying that commission towards closing costs or a reduction in list price.

Cons:

- Significant time investment to complete the licensing course and applicable tests;

- Significant cost to "activate" your license with a local broker. Usually $2,000+/year;

- It takes time, effort, and exposure to various situations in order to achieve a similar level of expertise as a great real estate agent.

If you are committed to creating a life through real estate as I have, knock yourself out. Get your license. If you would rather continue to serve in the military or remain in your current field of employment while utilizing the tools and tactics outlined in this book to achieve great wealth over time, that's a great path as well. An option for married couples that I've seen yield a lot of success is for one spouse to continue on the career path which provides a stable income, benefits, and a path to a pension or retirement plan, while the other spouse dives into real estate full time as an agent or investor.

Your Loan Officer

In a previous chapter, we discussed obtaining a mortgage loan, specifically a VA Loan. Your loan officer is the team member who will facilitate this process for you. The loan officer can work for a bank or for a mortgage brokerage company. You will have a flurry of communication with your loan officer and their team members early in the process to get all of your documents in order and issue your "pre-approval letter."

Here is a short list of common items, though often, there are other requirements that vary based on individual circumstances:

- Certificate of Eligibility from the Department of Veterans Affairs
- 2 years tax returns
- LES (active duty) or pay stubs to verify income
- Credit report

Here is an example of a pre-approval letter:

Banking Unusual

(Date)

RE: Mr. & Mrs. John Doe

Loan Type: (Conventional/ VA/ FHA...)

Congratulations! You have been Pre-Approved for a Mortgage Loan with Peoples Bank based on the following loan conditions:

1) Re-verification of your income, assets, liabilities and employment and that no material changes have occurred in your financial condition or creditworthiness prior to closing.
2) This approval is for a conventional 30 year fixed rate loan with a 20% down payment and a maximum purchase price of $600,000. An interest rate used for qualification was 3.75%. The total PITI not to exceed $2,250 and total loan amount not to exceed $525,000.
3) Receipt of standard closing documentation, i.e. acceptable appraisal, clear merchantable title to the property, survey, termite if applicable, final inspection, homeowners insurance, or other inspections as required.
4) Satisfactory verification of source of and existence of sufficient funds to close, including if applicable, documentation of gift funds, debt payoff and/or sale of current residence in order to receive cash needed for closing. Other documentation as requested may be reviewed prior to closing.
5) Confirmation prior to closing of satisfaction of the above conditions by Peoples Bank.

Thank you for allowing us to be a part of this important financial investment. If you have any questions regarding this pre-approval contact (Mortgage Loan Officer Name and title) at Peoples Bank by calling xxx-xxx-xxxx. This pre-approval expires 90 days from issuance and is subject to industry guideline changes. This letter does not constitute a contract and any rights related to this letter are not assignable and no third parties may rely on this letter.

(Mortgage Loan Officer Name)
(Title)
(Phone number)

Although a pre-approval letter isn't a formal loan approval, it's a fairly good indicator that you will qualify for the loan in the amount listed on your letter once you have selected a property and signed a contract with the seller.

Similar to your real estate agent, the loan officer is paid on commission based on sales (loans) they "originate." Loan origination is the entire loan process, from obtaining a pre-approval letter all the way through the actual funding of the loan at closing. Unlike your real estate agent, you are absolutely paying for this service, though perhaps not directly. The good news is that by law, the lender has to disclose the fees they are charging, as well as other costs to close the purchase of the property, on a form called the "loan estimate" or "good faith estimate."

Here is an example of a loan estimate:[1]

FICUS BANK
4321 Random Boulevard • Somecity, ST 12340

Save this Loan Estimate to compare with your Closing Disclosure.

Loan Estimate

DATE ISSUED	2/15/2013
APPLICANTS	Michael Jones and Mary Stone 123 Anywhere Street Anytown, ST 12345
PROPERTY	456 Somewhere Avenue Anytown, ST 12345
SALE PRICE	$180,000

LOAN TERM	30 years
PURPOSE	Purchase
PRODUCT	Fixed Rate
LOAN TYPE	☒ Conventional ☐ FHA ☐ VA ☐ _____
LOAN ID #	123456789
RATE LOCK	☐ NO ☒ YES, until 4/16/2013 at 5:00 p.m. EDT Before closing, your interest rate, points, and lender credits can change unless you lock the interest rate. All other estimated closing costs expire on 3/4/2013 at 5:00 p.m. EDT

Loan Terms

		Can this amount increase after closing?
Loan Amount	$162,000	NO
Interest Rate	3.875%	NO
Monthly Principal & Interest See Projected Payments below for your Estimated Total Monthly Payment	$761.78	NO

		Does the loan have these features?
Prepayment Penalty		YES • As high as $3,240 if you pay off the loan during the first 2 years
Balloon Payment		NO

Projected Payments

Payment Calculation	Years 1-7	Years 8-30
Principal & Interest	$761.78	$761.78
Mortgage Insurance	+ 82	+ —
Estimated Escrow Amount can increase over time	+ 206	+ 206
Estimated Total Monthly Payment	**$1,050**	**$968**

Estimated Taxes, Insurance & Assessments Amount can increase over time	$206 a month	This estimate includes ☒ Property Taxes ☒ Homeowner's Insurance ☐ Other: See Section G on page 2 for escrowed property costs. You must pay for other property costs separately.	In escrow? YES YES

Costs at Closing

Estimated Closing Costs	$8,054	Includes $5,672 in Loan Costs + $2,382 in Other Costs – $0 in Lender Credits. See page 2 for details.
Estimated Cash to Close	$16,054	Includes Closing Costs. See Calculating Cash to Close on page 2 for details.

Visit www.consumerfinance.gov/mortgage-estimate for general information and tools.

LOAN ESTIMATE PAGE 1 OF 3 • LOAN ID # 123456789

---

[1] https://www.consumerfinance.gov/owning-a-home/loan-estimate/

Closing Cost Details

Loan Costs

A. Origination Charges		$1,802
.25 % of Loan Amount (Points)		$405
Application Fee		$300
Underwriting Fee		$1,097

B. Services You Cannot Shop For		$672
Appraisal Fee		$405
Credit Report Fee		$30
Flood Determination Fee		$20
Flood Monitoring Fee		$32
Tax Monitoring Fee		$75
Tax Status Research Fee		$110

C. Services You Can Shop For		$3,198
Pest Inspection Fee		$135
Survey Fee		$65
Title – Insurance Binder		$700
Title – Lender's Title Policy		$535
Title – Settlement Agent Fee		$502
Title – Title Search		$1,261

D. TOTAL LOAN COSTS (A + B + C)	$5,672

Other Costs

E. Taxes and Other Government Fees		$85
Recording Fees and Other Taxes		$85
Transfer Taxes		

F. Prepaids		$867
Homeowner's Insurance Premium (6 months)		$605
Mortgage Insurance Premium (months)		
Prepaid Interest ($17.44 per day for 15 days @ 3.875%)		$262
Property Taxes (months)		

G. Initial Escrow Payment at Closing		$413
Homeowner's Insurance	$100.83 per month for 2 mo.	$202
Mortgage Insurance	per month for mo.	
Property Taxes	$105.30 per month for 2 mo.	$211

H. Other		$1,017
Title – Owner's Title Policy (optional)		$1,017

I. TOTAL OTHER COSTS (E + F + G + H)	$2,382

J. TOTAL CLOSING COSTS		$8,054
D + I		$8,054
Lender Credits		

Calculating Cash to Close

Total Closing Costs (J)	$8,054
Closing Costs Financed (Paid from your Loan Amount)	$0
Down Payment/Funds from Borrower	$18,000
Deposit	– $10,000
Funds for Borrower	$0
Seller Credits	$0
Adjustments and Other Credits	$0
Estimated Cash to Close	$16,054

Additional Information About This Loan

LENDER	Ficus Bank	**MORTGAGE BROKER**	
NMLS/_LICENSE ID		**NMLS/_LICENSE ID**	
LOAN OFFICER	Joe Smith	**LOAN OFFICER**	
NMLS/_LICENSE ID	12345	**NMLS/_LICENSE ID**	
EMAIL	joesmith@ficusbank.com	**EMAIL**	
PHONE	123-456-7890	**PHONE**	

Comparisons — Use these measures to compare this loan with other loans.

In 5 Years	$56,582	Total you will have paid in principal, interest, mortgage insurance, and loan costs.
	$15,773	Principal you will have paid off.
Annual Percentage Rate (APR)	4.274%	Your costs over the loan term expressed as a rate. This is not your interest rate.
Total Interest Percentage (TIP)	69.45%	The total amount of interest that you will pay over the loan term as a percentage of your loan amount.

Other Considerations

Appraisal	We may order an appraisal to determine the property's value and charge you for this appraisal. We will promptly give you a copy of any appraisal, even if your loan does not close. You can pay for an additional appraisal for your own use at your own cost.
Assumption	If you sell or transfer this property to another person, we ☐ will allow, under certain conditions, this person to assume this loan on the original terms. ☒ will not allow assumption of this loan on the original terms.
Homeowner's Insurance	This loan requires homeowner's insurance on the property, which you may obtain from a company of your choice that we find acceptable.
Late Payment	If your payment is more than 15 days late, we will charge a late fee of 5% of the monthly principal and interest payment.
Refinance	Refinancing this loan will depend on your future financial situation, the property value, and market conditions. You may not be able to refinance this loan.
Servicing	We intend ☐ to service your loan. If so, you will make your payments to us. ☒ to transfer servicing of your loan.

Confirm Receipt

By signing, you are only confirming that you have received this form. You do not have to accept this loan because you have signed or received this form.

_____   _____   _____   _____
Applicant Signature   Date   Co-Applicant Signature   Date

LOAN ESTIMATE

Often, real estate agents work closely with mortgage loan officers. It is advisable to interview your real estate agent's preferred lender. It is likely they do a decent job, or your real estate agent would have dumped them!

Do not feel obligated to use the mortgage loan officer that your real estate agent prefers, however. Oftentimes, agents and loan officers share marketing platforms and "leads" which can create a potential conflict of interest: the real estate agent is going to get a commission from your sale, but they get a steady flow of new buyers from that mortgage loan officer.

Most real estate agents and mortgage loan officers are good people, but they are just that, people. It's human nature that a real estate agent or lender could look the other way if something isn't quite right with your purchase or loan in order to obtain their own commission. I don't bring this up to make you paranoid of the motives of those on your team, but it is wise to acknowledge their goals as well as your own and keep watch. You are the OIC and need to understand the dynamics that exist within your home buying team so you can best manage them in order to achieve your goal.

Issuing VA Loans is big business. Last year, more than 600,000 VA Loans were issued to veterans across the country. With big business comes big marketing and tactics that aren't completely honest. Here are the two that really bother me:

1. Lenders' advertisements that insinuate that they "are" the VA. Or that they are the "only" ones who can offer you a VA Loan. As covered previously, the Department of Veterans Affairs does not lend money; the banks do. The VA simply guarantees a portion of the total debt, which allows the banks to cater to a wider credit profile and offer better rates to VA borrowers.

2. Institutions who offer a "rebate" of some kind when you obtain a loan with them. The government can create money out of thin air, unlike the rest of us. So, this "rebate" comes from somewhere, or rather, someone. The most likely sources are either a portion of your real estate agent's commission or higher fees on your loan estimate in other areas of the transaction.

Competition is the American way, so obtain quotes from several banks or mortgage brokers and keep them honest! Your lender doesn't necessarily have to be local, but I've found it's helpful to be able to go to their office and meet face to face, especially if the purchase hits a speed bump along the way. In my experience, mortgage brokers tend to outperform banks in timeliness of closing (you don't want to be the person with the moving truck parked in front of the house that isn't yours yet!) and also in overall cost, because they are shopping multiple lending sources to find the most attractive terms for you.

In a perfect world, the mortgage lender that your agent has a relationship with will offer the lowest cost, the best service, and have the highest probability of closing on time without issue. However, you are in charge and need to take the loan process as seriously as you do the selection of the property. There is a lot of money that can be lost by blindly accepting the first loan proposal you receive. Take a look at this chart:

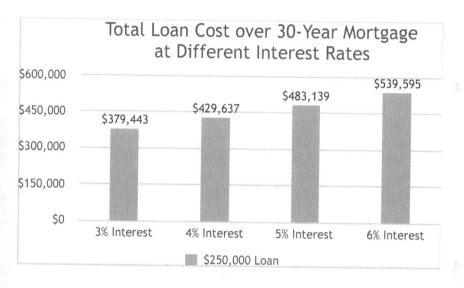

Home Inspector

Unless you are an undiscovered Chip or Joanna Gaines from HGTV, you absolutely must have a home inspection. Unless you don't like money. It does you absolutely no good to obtain a property with $0 down if you move in and incur massive costs to fix something that would have been discovered by spending a few hundred bucks to have the property professionally inspected.

One of my SWCC buddies called me (after using another real estate agent to purchase the property, ahem) in a panic when he got around to investigating why the floors were all sloping towards the dock in his backyard. It was discovered that due to his failure to obtain a proper inspection during his due diligence, he (and the VA appraiser—they tend not to go underneath houses) missed $50,000 in termite and fungus damage, along with a shifting foundation. Again, a $0 down VA Loan doesn't do you much good if you have to cough up $50,000 in cash to restore the structural integrity of the house you bought.

Your real estate agent will likely have several referrals for home inspectors they've worked with successfully in the past. Their referral, along with a web search to search reviews is a great place to start to find a quality home inspector. Here are a few suggestions to protect yourself when selecting a home inspector:

- Verify they are licensed and insured
- Select a home inspector who is certified with the American Society of Home Inspectors
- Avoid home inspectors who also run contracting companies (potential conflict of interest).

In addition to a standard home inspection, certain properties may require additional inspections such as:

- Termite
- Moisture
- Lead based paint (properties built before 1978)
- Radon gas
- Well
- Septic
- Oil Tank

- Chimney

- Pool

It is important not to be alarmist when reviewing inspection reports, while at the same time addressing any significant issues that could affect your safety, the structure, and the proper operation of major systems within the property. The VA appraisal is required to protect the bank and the VA, but it protects you as well. They will flag major issues they see for repair. The appraiser is a human being and it's possible for them to make a mistake. They also don't go into as much detail with their inspection as your hired home inspector will. Take full advantage of your physical due diligence or "inspection" time frame and get a home inspection. Don't end up like my SWCC buddy and his huge bill!

If there are issues, you'll need your next team member, the General Contractor.

General Contractor

This team member may not be required for all purchases, but it is better to have them lined up and not need them, rather than need them and not know where to find them. You General Contractor or "GC" is your one stop shop for home improvement. They might not specialize in every trade or element of construction, but they will hire and manage experts on your behalf if they need to "subcontract" any of the work you require.

Your GC is similar to your real estate agent in the sense that you are relying on their expertise to get your desired outcome. Finding quality tradesmen, just like finding quality properties, can be very difficult. The General Contractor takes care of this for you.

If the home inspection didn't go so well, it's best to obtain quotes of your own before sending a repair request list back to the seller. This way, you know exactly what you're asking of them and you're in a better position to negotiate.

Phil Capron

I've flipped a lot of houses and have sold a lot of houses others have flipped. A common tactic used by flippers is to leave a "red herring" or two that they were planning on fixing anyway, but they left for your home inspection to catch. Make sure you are addressing the most serious (structure, safety, major systems) in your repair addendum you send back to the seller and obtain quotes for those things. Don't be distracted by the obvious red herrings that are easy fixes and don't jeopardize the safety, structural, or mechanical integrity of the property.

Depending on how handy or stubborn you are, you may elect to do some repairs or home improvement yourself. If the scope of work involves electrical, plumbing, roofing, major systems, or another specialized knowledge and certification, please consult a professional.

Managing people is difficult when they don't have to worry about being court martialed for disobeying you. Contractors are notoriously difficult to coordinate and hold to a standard for their work. If they weren't, half the people I know would be multimillionaires from flipping houses. Finding a General Contractor, you can trust to conduct the work required on time and on budget can be the difference between a great buy and a huge headache.

We are seeking properties at a discount, and one key differentiator between properties sold at market price and those sold for less is property condition. Ideally, we can find a property with the classic "good bones" that just needs a little TLC. The VA Appraiser isn't going to allow the purchase of a property with major defects, but items like old carpet, ugly wallpaper, or an outdated kitchen or bathrooms could get you the discount from market price you're seeking. If you are planning on "forcing appreciation" or raising the value through "sweat equity" with physical improvements to the property, it is best to understand what is required in time, labor, and capital (money) during your inspection period. Here are a few questions you should ask prospective contractors before hiring them:

- How long have you been in business?

- Are you licensed and insured? May I see proof of both?

- May I contact three of your previous clients who hired you for similar jobs?

- What is the timeline for my job? What happens if it isn't met?

- What happens if we go over budget from our contract price?

Title Company/Closing Attorney

Depending on where you are purchasing a property, you will either use a Title Company or Closing Attorney. These two terms are interchangeable for our purposes. Technically, the Title Company is the one who is providing "title insurance" to both the buyer and lender, and a Real Estate Closing Attorney is the one who conducts the actual closing of the property. Often, title companies have in-house attorneys to facilitate real estate closings and act as counsel for the title company. More important than getting their name correct is understanding what the title company and/or closing attorney are actually doing for you, the buyer.

Usually, you will engage this team member immediately after conducting your inspections and you are certain you are proceeding with the purchase. In my experience, it is better to wait to start with title work until after inspections as this phase also costs money. It would be a shame to spend the money for a title search and other fees only to find out the property didn't pass your physical, financial, or neighborhood inspection. Once you get to this point of the transaction, what does this team member actually do for you? Here are a few things:

- What does the Closing Attorney do?
    - Perform a "title search" which ensures that the seller has the legal right to transfer the property (they are the legal owner), that there are not any open "judgements" (lawsuits, contractors that have not been paid for work on the house, et cetera.), and that there are no additional mortgages on the property;

- Orders the property "survey," which ensures the property boundaries are respected by the subject property and neighbors, and will uncover any "easements" (rights to access the property) by utility companies or other parties

- Ensures the elements of the contract are enforced at closing;

- "Escrows" or holds your "Earnest Money Deposit" and distributes funds post-closing to seller, buyer, real estate brokers, and other parties paid on the settlement statement.

Your real estate agent is a great resource for referrals to great title companies or real estate attorneys. Just like the mortgage lender, it is important to work with a company who has a great track record of delivering on their promises.

There are many moving parts involved in getting a real estate contract to a successful closing, so don't take this team member for granted. Communicate early and often with them (possibly through your real estate agent) to make sure they are on track to achieve your desired closing date, and always leave a little buffer in your plans, just in case.

CPA

It's not the most entertaining topic, but taxes are your #1 expense and worthy of discussion and expert counsel. Your Certified Public Accountant is your defender and not only helps you keep more of your hard-earned money, but also shields you from a lot of the aggravation and painstaking time spent filing your own taxes. In my opinion, the services of an expert are well worth the expense for peace of mind alone.

A great CPA will analyze your income, expenses, and tax exposure to recommend the optimal strategy for your individual situation. If you're early in your military career, your taxes likely won't be that complex. As you acquire properties and other investments, and move through the ranks and earn more money, your tax situation will change. It is critical to obtain the professional counsel of a CPA as you progress, but I think it's a great idea to start out with one no matter your rank or income.

Now that your team is assembled, and you know the nine line for the VA Loan process, you're ready to hit the ground running, right? Not so fast... we know that buying "something" and allowing the forces of real estate to work for us over time, will work. It's just math. However, I don't think you took the time to read this book and otherwise educate yourself simply to buy "something." Let's take a look at what's required to buy the "right thing." This extra effort will pay off in spades by removing as many of the elements of "luck" (market fluctuation) as possible and ensuring we are making this big decision with eyes wide open.

Chapter Six:

What Am I Buying?

Have you ever heard the old adage that you want to buy "the worst house in the best neighborhood?" There is some truth to that statement, but it's not the entire story. Before jumping in and signing your name on hundreds of thousands of dollars of debt, it is wise to make sure you understand exactly what you're buying. You're not only buying a house, you're buying a neighborhood, and a market.

The House

The house is as far as most buyers go. Once they find "the one," they'll overlook deficiencies in the neighborhood and the market in order to get their dream structure. We'll take a look at the other factors, but we'll address the right house first since it seems like that's where everyone wants to start! It is critically important that during our journey we don't just buy anything, we want to make sure to buy the right thing. What exactly does that mean? The following goals, while not absolute as every situation is different, are a good place to start.

10% Below Market Value

10% may seem like a fairly arbitrary number, but there is some method to my madness. Previously we discussed how great it is to be a buyer with a VA Loan, because all of your costs can be covered if executed correctly. That means 0% down on the mortgage, the seller pays the real estate agent commissions, and you receive a credit for "closing cost assistance" to cover costs like your loan fees, appraisal, inspection, survey, etc. What a deal! When you become the seller, guess who's paying for all of the items you took advantage of when you purchased the property? You guessed it. You are. Here's a quick example of how the fees break down as a seller assuming a $200,000 sales price.

Sales Price	$200,000
Real Estate Commissions (6%)	-$12,000
Buyer's Closing Costs (3%)	-$6,000
Seller's Closing Costs (1%)	-$2,000
Total Proceeds	**$180,000**

In this example, if you had purchased the property at a 10% discount at the time of purchase and were forced to sell due to a PCS or other life event shortly thereafter, you should be able to escape without bringing money to the closing table. It is always my intention to be a real estate buyer, not a real estate seller, but sometimes life happens. It sure is nice to have this 10% equity buffer built in at the time of purchase. Since real estate markets are imperfect, there are opportunities to negotiate discounts of 10% or more. Finding (or more likely creating) those opportunities is a mixture between art and science. The science is fairly straightforward. How does the property stack up against others that are on the market and have recently sold? Will it rent for more than the monthly obligations "as is"? The art has to do with dealing with other humans (negotiation) and understanding what people are looking for in housing. It also has a lot to do with reading the tea leaves regarding trends within a market.

Opportunities for a Discount

When it comes to negotiation, the party who needs to make a deal is always in the weaker negotiating position. It always bothered me when I worked as a real estate agent and I heard other agents talk about their military buyer who was PCSing and "had to have a contract this weekend." If the buyer's agent keeps it to themselves as they should, the damage is minimal... but operating under those time constraints is no way to set yourself up for success. If that piece of information makes its way to the listing agent representing the seller however, the buyer's negotiation power is eviscerated. As a buyer, you want to maintain the position that you want a house, but you don't need it. Once you set your criteria with your real estate agent, do not deviate for the sake of expediency. The seller has to sell, you don't have to buy. If the seller doesn't need to sell, it's unlikely we will achieve the kind of discount we are seeking with them in order to purchase their property.

If I had to choose one word to describe how I find real estate opportunities it would be "Distress." We are seeking sellers who due to life circumstances are distressed and properties whose conditions are distressed. A recurring theme in this book is deciding whether to hit the easy button and stay within our comfort zone, or to put in a little more effort for a much greater result over the long-term. Dealing with distress as it pertains to real estate is definitely the more difficult path, but the dividends are well worth it.

Here's a quick story about how distress made me and my partners $1,500,000 in one deal. While this isn't a VA Loan story, it illustrates the power of distress and how to capitalize on inefficient markets in order to negotiate the best possible deal. Remember that inefficient markets are those in which asset prices are not reflective of their actual value. Because of this fact, great deals can be created in this business.

I was searching for my next apartment building and noticed a large portfolio of properties listed at a fair price in one of my target markets. After conducting some quick due diligence about the offering, I phoned the broker to see what else I could find out about the listing.

Whenever I make these phone calls, I'm searching for what Chris Voss, former Chief Hostage Negotiator for the FBI, refers to as the "black swan" in his amazing book *Never Split the Difference*. The "black swan," according to Voss, is the one piece of information that once discovered, changes the entire face of the negotiation.

In this case, I found out that the properties had been listed for some time, and had actually had a contract and that the buyer failed to proceed to closing due to items discovered during the property inspection. Naturally, the seller was frustrated that they had negotiated a contract and the buyer backed out. I also learned that the seller was the heir of the original owner and didn't have any interest in continuing to own the properties. Early in the discovery phase and preliminary negotiation, I'd already found three elements of seller distress.

- A previous contract had failed to close due to property condition
- The seller inherited the properties
- The seller had no desire to own the properties and wanted out

In addition to the fantastic information I'd received about the seller's situation, there was one more element of distress. Unlike the previous items that impacted the seller, this new piece of information was actually something that impacted the potential buyers of these properties. The properties were listed as a portfolio, including several buildings in different locations. This presented problems to the buyer for obtaining financing on the properties, as well as making the future management of the properties difficult as they were not all in one central location. With this information in mind, I toured the properties, engaged in negotiations, and ultimately contracted to buy the buildings. My partners and I were thrilled when the appraisal came in $1,500,000 higher than our contract price!

While there are vast differences between a single-family home that you intend to occupy and a large apartment portfolio, the underlying pain points that enabled me to create such a great deal are the same. When you find a property owner who doesn't want to own their property, who can't afford to maintain their property, or is dealing with a life event that is taking them away from the property, it's very possible that you've uncovered a gold mine. The two key areas of distress are seller distress and property distress. Let's take a look at both.

Seller Distress- Types of Sellers

Real Estate Owned (REO)

Banks and other noteholders that have foreclosed on real estate loans and physically taken the property back from the borrower. Banks are not in the business of owning property, so they wish to dispose of these assets as quickly as possible. Because of this fact, REO properties, more commonly known as "foreclosures" are often available for a discount. However, as you'll discover once you begin looking at properties and making offers, price is only one part of the total "deal" equation.

> *Beware: Banks usually sell their REO properties "as-is." If there are issues uncovered during the home inspection or appraisal, the bank usually will not fix them.*

You will have to rely on your real estate agent to guide you to bank owned properties that are in acceptable condition, and owned by banks who are willing to work with buyers utilizing a VA Loan. Some banks will only entertain "non contingent" or "as-is" offers, which won't work for our strategy. The risk is too high. There are actually some banks and government institutions that mandate "owner occupants" (this is you!) get a certain period of time to make offers on their properties before "investors." Your real estate agent will help you navigate these waters and identify the available REO opportunities in your market.

Short Sales

A "short sale" is when a homeowner petitions the bank to accept a payoff at closing of less than what is owed on their mortgage note. Why would the bank accept less? Simply put, foreclosing on a real estate loan is really, really, really expensive. Because of this fact, some lenders choose to negotiate a short sale rather than deal with many months of nonpayment by the borrower (loan default) and the astronomical attorney fees incurred to reclaim the property. The short sale process can be bewildering to the unindoctrinated. Here is a simplified step by step process:

1. The buyer submits an offer to the homeowner (seller).
2. The seller accepts the offer (or counters and the buyer accepts the counter).
3. A "short sale negotiator" (often a real estate closing attorney) assists the seller in submitting documentation required by the bank in order to review their petition for short sale.
4. The bank accepts the contract and short sale, rejects the contract and short sale, or counters the contract back to the buyer.
5. In the event of a counter by the bank, buyer decides whether to accept the counter offer or release their contract with the homeowner.
6. Once an agreement has been reached between buyer and seller that is agreeable to the bank (who authorizes the short sale) the transaction can proceed to closing.

Short sales can definitely be confusing. They also take a long time to close due to the "third party approval," which is the bank consenting to the transaction closing for an amount less than what is owed. I have purchased short sales that I'd had under contract for so many months that I'd forgotten about the contract when the short sale negotiator or listing agent called to inform me that the short sale had been approved. As an agent, I had a short sale listing under contract for two years before the bank agreed to sell it at those terms instead of foreclosing on the property, it was unbelievable! Short sales are not for the faint of heart.

I love short sales, some of my best deals have been short sales and I've helped numerous clients acquire property with a solid equity position by purchasing properties this way. As previously mentioned, you never want to be in the position that you "need" to buy a property. If you do need to buy a property, do not submit an offer on a short sale.

Just like REOs, you will rely on your real estate agent to best advise you when it comes to these distressed properties, but here are a couple tips to achieve short sale success:

1. Only work with listing agents who understand short sales and have engaged a professional short sale negotiator to handle correspondence with the bank.
2. Make sure your home inspection, appraisal, title search, and due diligence (inspection) timelines begin when "third party approval is delivered to the buyer in writing" and not immediately after the contract is written, like a normal purchase.

Estate Sales

Estates are a sad but very common reality in every market. When a homeowner passes away, their house will often be sold soon thereafter. It's a stressful time for the family, and often they just want a quick sale or for a new individual or family to make the now vacant house into a home again. Often these properties are outdated which may be a turnoff to other buyers in the marketplace. Remember that we are looking for properties with great bones. You can fix cosmetic issues and make the property your own over time. The important thing is to buy the property with built in equity, and estate sales are a great opportunity to achieve that goal.

Property Distress

Vacant Properties

If a property is vacant, the seller is experiencing the pain of paying their mortgage, taxes, insurance, and general upkeep of the property without any income to offset those expenses. Even if the property is owned "free and clear," meaning that there is no longer a mortgage encumbering the property, the taxes and other expenses related to keeping and maintaining the property do not stop. Some vacant property owners may have already relocated to their new home and now paying a double mortgage payment every month! Owners of vacant properties definitely have a strong incentive to strike a deal. Your real estate agent will love it when you request to tour vacant properties, as they are the easiest to show. Usually, it's a quick online request or call to the listing agent and you'll be approved for a tour shortly thereafter.

Properties Occupied by Tenants

Some of my least favorite experiences as a real estate agent were showing, or attempting to show, properties occupied by tenants. When a homeowner who still occupies their home is informed that a prospective buyer has scheduled a tour, they usually roll out the red carpet. The house will be clean, the lights will be on, scented candles will infuse the property with various scents, it's like watching a home buying show on HGTV. The owner will do anything to make the house feel like home to the new buyer, their bottom line depends on it!

A tenant occupied house will often show like the polar opposite when compared to the pretty picture painted above. From the tenants' perspective, they're paying rent, they are likely unhappy they're going to be relocated soon, and they don't have a lot of reasons to cooperate with the sale of the property. A humorous example of tenants interfering with a sale is found in the movie *Step Brothers*. I've never seen anything quite like that in real life, but it doesn't shock me when I hear tenant horror stories from other agents or investors regarding tenants' antics.

When you tour a tenant-occupied property, it will usually be very apparent based on the condition of the property. Tenants also have the tendency to cancel showings, not vacate the premises in order for the buyer to tour, and to otherwise gum up the works. This can be an opportunity for you if you can look past their behavior, junk, and cleanliness, and instead focus on the house itself. Chances are the seller may be frustrated due to poor showing feedback from their listing agent. This can result in the resetting of pricing expectations even if a formal price reduction isn't advertised through the MLS. If a property shows poorly due to a tenant, but otherwise meets your criteria, consider putting in an offer based on what you can see. The worst they can say is no.

Stigmatized Properties

How brave are you? Stigmatized properties are properties in which some taboo or undesirable occurrence has taken place. Common examples of property stigma are crime, a death in the property, or supernatural events. Disclosure requirements of potential stigmas vary by state, so ask your real estate agent about the possibility of finding a stigmatized property in your market. The stigma refers to what has happened in the property, the actual property may be in great shape! Finding a stigmatized property is a lot less common than finding a REO or short sale, but they present the potential to negotiate a great deal, if you dare!

Outdated Properties: Ugly Ducklings

It's fun and easy to look at the new construction and "flip" properties that hit the market, but we aren't able to acquire them at a discount. I've sold a lot of flip and new construction houses to military members, but before doing so we had a long talk. I made sure they understood they were exposing themselves to market forces going the wrong way in the short-term. I let them know that being able to sell for a profit or even a break-even amount over the next few years might be impossible. Ultimately, they decided that the pretty house was the best option for their family and went through with the purchases. As long as our service members and veterans are making these purchases with eyes wide open, and contingency plans as well as adequate capital reserves (money) are in place, so be it. This is the most common recipe for financial disaster using a VA loan, so beware! *(steps down from soapbox)*

Being a recovering flipper myself, I understand what flippers require in order to make their margins. Generally, flippers want to acquire properties at 70% of the fair market value of the property minus the repairs required to transform it into one of the best homes in the neighborhood. It's extremely rare for a homeowner doing a traditional sale with a real estate agent to be able to offer the discount required for a flipper to be interested, since they require such a large delta between purchase price and their ultimate sale price to an end buyer. This fact combined with the tendency of most "regular" home buyers to go for the most updated property they can afford creates a void in the market for ugly ducklings.

If you can find a property with solid bones and mechanical systems that just needs cosmetic updates in order to make it a swan, you may have found an opportunity to negotiate some equity on the purchase. With a little vision, creativity, and elbow grease, you'll be able to make it your own and increase the value through "forced appreciation" or "sweat equity." The combination of dialing in on an ugly duckling and having the foresight to make it into a swan can do wonders for your equity position in the property and will ensure it rents quickly and for more money than if you hadn't updated the cosmetic aspects of the property.

In commercial real estate, like the apartment buildings I buy, we call adding value through physical improvements "forced appreciation." In the residential real estate space, it's more commonly referred to as "sweat equity." It's much more common for the owner to do some of the non-skilled work themselves on a residential property, hence the "sweat" part of the saying. There are so many great advantages to real estate, it's hard to pick one as my favorite, but forcing appreciation on the properties I own is the aspect I enjoy most because I control it. Utilizing my skills to identify improvements that will add value and executing them is a lot more gratifying than amortization or appreciation over time, because I was the variable that resulted in success If I wanted to invest based on what I cannot control, I'd just invest in the stock market. It may sound like a major undertaking, but you can do what I do, starting with your first purchase. Here is a quick example:

You purchase a house as an estate sale that was originally listed for $190,000. You negotiated a discount because the heirs to the estate didn't have any use for it and didn't want to continue making a mortgage payment every month. You were able to purchase the property using your VA Loan for $160,000. It has 4 bedrooms and 2 full bathrooms, is 1,500 square feet, has a one car garage, and sits on a nice lot in a desirable neighborhood in which other comparable homes sell between $190,000 and $220,000. Structurally, the house is in good shape with a roof that has been replaced in the last 5 years, it has good windows, satisfactory plumbing and electrical, and a HVAC system in good repair.

The feedback the listing agent received from the other buyers who had toured the property was negative, as the previous owner was a heavy smoker and all of the carpet was old and dirty. You decide to tackle the cosmetic items after closing, knowing that there is an opportunity to create some value with a little elbow grease. Here is your plan and budget:

Purchase Price		-$160,000
	New Flooring	-$6,000
	Paint	-$3,000
	Trash Out	-$1,000
Total Spent on the Home:		-$170,000
New Market Value		**$200,000**

In the above example, a little sweat equity and $10,000 was able to unlock $30,000 in additional equity in the property, as well as give you a like new property to enjoy. Your General Contractor is a great resource for the cost of repairs in your area. However, all of the work listed above can be done by an enterprising home owner without a contractor. One of my favorite repairs is when a property has a smoke or pet smell. Air purification machines, removing the old carpet, and painting over everything with primer does wonders in eliminating unpleasant odors and making a property feel new again.

During your search, you're likely to encounter properties with pet odors, smoke, ugly carpet, ugly wallpaper, or a host of other undesirable cosmetic items. While these issues cause others to run for the front door, I invite you to view them as opportunities to negotiate a great deal. To the uninitiated, a smoker's home or one with pet odors smells bad, but many investors remark that it "smells like money!" upon walking through the front door. I invite you to train your brain (and your nose!) to be those of an investor, not a consumer.

Functionally Obsolete Properties

Beauty is in the eye of the beholder when it comes to trends, but functionality is another matter altogether. Functional obsolescence occurs when a property lacks a feature that current buyers are looking for in a property. For example, if you have two kids, a boy and a girl, and want them to each have their own bedroom, a 2-bedroom home simply will not work for you. It lacks the functionality (three bedrooms) that you require. The same can be said about the number of bathrooms, having a master bath, a garage or off-street parking, or even a fenced backyard. If there is a feature that most buyers are demanding in the current market that a particular property lacks, it is functionally obsolete.

The key when taking a look at a functionally obsolete property is asking "can this functional obsolescence be cured?" This example is a little out there, but imagine you found a house with no bathroom, but it had an outhouse. I'd say that would qualify as "functionally obsolete" to most people. Because of that fact, the property is only listed at $100,000 when the neighboring properties all sell for $200,000 plus. Through one of our trusted team members, our General Contractor, we learn we could add a bathroom to the house for

$20,000. Would you invest $20,000 on an improvement that would create a $100,000 in equity? I most certainly would!

The outhouse example is a little outlandish, but illustrative nonetheless. Let's take a look at some potential items of functional obsolescence that can be cured.

- **2-bedroom properties:** Properties that are only listed as 2-bedroom can often be converted to 3-bedroom houses with minimal effort. I had one client who bought a 2-bedroom home that had another room listed as an office. All the office lacked was a closet to be considered a bedroom. They realized this and added the closet, which made the property much more valuable!
- **Choppy floor plans:** Lots of buyers today are looking for an open concept. Many older homes have sectioned off, choppy floor plans. However, with so many walls, it is probable that not all of them are load bearing. Your General Contractor will be able to tell you which walls are structural, and which ones are just 2x4s and drywall. If there is a big difference in value between homes with an open concept and those with closed off floor plans, that fact might be the black swan you need to negotiate a great deal on the purchase. It could also give you the ability to create a lot of value by doing some surgery once you own the home.
- **Master bedroom without a master bath**: In many older homes, it is common for a bathroom to be shared between several bedrooms. If the bathroom shares a wall with the master bedroom, it may be possible to add a door for direct access from the master bedroom. It may not seem like a big deal, but for many buyers not having a bathroom attached is a huge turn off. If a doorway can be added connecting the master bedroom with the bathroom, it can add a lot of value to the property.
- **Garage conversions**: In some markets, buyers are not paying a premium for garages and homeowners elect to convert the garage space into living space. Whether it becomes an additional bedroom, rec room, or office is negotiable. This plan makes sense if the cost to convert is significantly less than the market price per square foot (your real estate agent can provide this data).

To recap, functionally obsolete properties are interesting to us as investment minded buyers for two reasons. Primarily, these properties will not receive as much buyer interest as more functional properties, which provides an opportunity to negotiate a discount. Secondarily, if the obsolescence can be cured for a low cost, we can create value through forced appreciation by correcting the undesirable aspects of a property or lack of functionality.

Viable Rentals

Because we prefer to be real estate buyers, not real estate sellers, it is important to address the implications of leaving the property before we buy it. We only want to purchase property that is a viable rental the day we buy it. Some of this analysis is more about the market as a whole and reading the tea leaves about what the future holds. Make no mistake, there can be tremendous variance from property to property even in the same neighborhood. As discussed in the chapter on building your team, now is the time to engage one or more local property managers to obtain their opinion on fair rental market value for the property in question.

Every market is different, so it is difficult for me to suggest a rule of thumb regarding what makes a good rental on the basis of "it makes X dollars more than the mortgage and expenses every month." However, I believe it is prudent at the absolute minimum to ensure the market rent is enough to pay for your mortgage, taxes, insurance, property management fees, and a small contribution to a "reserve fund" for repairs. It may not be for several years, but inevitably the property manager will need to order repairs on your behalf, it is wise to have a reserve fund set aside specifically for this purpose.

Remember the formula:

Rent-Mortgage-Other Expenses = CASH FLOW

Cash flow is king. We only want properties that have the ability to make cash flow for us as owners. Sophisticated investors with deep pockets sometimes violate this rule, but they have the experience to do so, and they usually have a very good reason! Since every market is different and cannot be compared apples to apples, here is a method that investors use to describe the rent compared to the total purchase price of a property. This can be used regardless of your market to compare potential properties.

A property purchased for $100,000 that rents for $1,000 is called a "1% property," as the monthly rent is equal to one percent of the purchase price. The higher the percentage, the higher the cash flow should be for a particular property. If the same $100,000 property rented for $1,500 per month, it would be a great deal as a "1.5% property." To take it one step further, if the same $100,000 property rented for $2,000 per month, we've hit the jackpot with a mythical "2% deal." As you are surfing properties on the internet or from your real estate agent's list, practice searching rental rates for comparable properties and do your own calculations. It's a simple procedure and very quickly you'll get an idea of the average ratio between the market rent and the purchase price.

Remember, the calculation is

$$Rent/Purchase\ Price = \_\_\%\ property$$

This may come as a surprise, but inexpensive properties tend to rent for a higher percentage than their higher-priced competition. When you think about it, it actually makes sense that there is a significant variance between economy housing and higher-end housing. The difference is due to who is renting these properties. On the lower end of the housing spectrum, the people renting those properties are very price-conscious. Often this is due to a financial or life circumstance that prevents them from buying their own home. Since their leverage, or negotiation power, in the market place is low (they don't have the option to buy a home), rents tend to be higher because the landlords know that. Just like the banks that charge the lion's share of the interest on the front half of the loan, landlords are taking advantage of simple supply and demand. It's the golden rule. "He who has the gold, makes the rule."

As you go up the housing food chain, renters have the option of mobility, they can shop around, and they can buy their own home if the rental rates become restrictive. Because of these market realities, the rent-to-purchase-price-ratio and thus the cash flow is actually inversely proportional to purchase price. Lower-priced properties tend to rent for more than their higher priced counterparts, pound for pound.

Price-to-Rent Ratio by City

According to SmartAsset.com, these are the price-to-rent ratios of every city in the US with a population over 250,000.[2] Here, the price-to-rent ratio is based on 12 months, so it's a little larger than the ratio I was discussing above. A "12" price-to-rent ratio is equal to a 1% Deal.

City	Price-to-Rent Ratio	Home Price (for a $1,000 Rental)
San Francisco, California	50.11	$601,362
Oakland, California	41.05	$492,611
Honolulu, Hawaii	39.50	$474,014
Los Angeles, California	38.59	$463,135
New York, New York	36.83	$441,987
Long Beach, California	36.37	$436,385
Seattle, Washington	36.07	$432,862
San Jose, California	33.77	$405,263
Washington, D.C.	33.76	$405,070
Anaheim, California	30.50	$365,970
San Diego, California	30.47	$365,591
Irvine, California	30.29	$363,439
Portland, Oregon	29.30	$351,563
Boston, Massachusetts	29.23	$350,811

---

[2] Find the full article at: https://smartasset.com/mortgage/price-to-rent-ratio-in-us-cities

City	Price-to-Rent Ratio	Home Price (for a $1,000 Rental)
Santa Ana, California	27.56	$330,682
Chula Vista, California	25.86	$310,349
Denver, Colorado	25.60	$307,232
Jersey City, New Jersey	23.66	$283,931
Miami, Florida	23.04	$276,481
Sacramento, California	23.04	$276,461
Riverside, California	22.72	$272,633
Atlanta, Georgia	22.60	$271,196
Austin, Texas	22.29	$267,444
Stockton, California	22.19	$266,289
Henderson, Nevada	21.12	$253,420
Minneapolis, Minnesota	21.10	$253,185
Anchorage, Alaska	20.66	$247,870
Fresno, California	20.48	$245,807
Colorado Springs, Colorado	20.23	$242,818
Plano, Texas	20.03	$240,336
Chicago, Illinois	19.99	$239,831
New Orleans, Louisiana	19.73	$236,798
Albuquerque, New Mexico	19.60	$235,245
Chandler, Arizona	19.46	$233,493
Las Vegas, Nevada	19.10	$229,225
Nashville, Tennessee	19.06	$228,730
Phoenix, Arizona	19.00	$228,036
Durham, North Carolina	18.91	$226,923
Aurora, Colorado	18.90	$226,798

City	Price-to-Rent Ratio	Home Price (for a $1,000 Rental)
Lexington, Kentucky	18.84	$226,112
Mesa, Arizona	18.67	$224,028
St. Paul, Minnesota	18.56	$222,679
Raleigh, North Carolina	18.46	$221,534
Bakersfield, California	18.46	$221,534
Newark, New Jersey	18.42	$221,072
Madison, Wisconsin	18.32	$219,817
Tampa, Florida	18.01	$216,081
Virginia Beach, Virginia	17.81	$213,702
Lincoln, Nebraska	17.45	$209,413
Cincinnati, Ohio	17.11	$205,308
Orlando, Florida	16.83	$201,910
Louisville, Kentucky	16.51	$198,148
Charlotte, North Carolina	16.51	$198,070
Dallas, Texas	16.01	$192,137
Greensboro, North Carolina	15.84	$190,073
Oklahoma City, Oklahoma	15.68	$188,109
Tucson, Arizona	15.34	$184,088
St. Petersburg, Florida	15.27	$183,195
St. Louis, Missouri	15.13	$181,515
Jacksonville, Florida	14.93	$179,150
Omaha, Nebraska	14.68	$176,121
Houston, Texas	14.67	$176,065
Tulsa, Oklahoma	14.35	$172,256
Wichita, Kansas	14.32	$171,883

City	Price-to-Rent Ratio	Home Price (for a $1,000 Rental)
Philadelphia, Pennsylvania	14.29	$171,517
Fort Worth, Texas	14.20	$170,423
Arlington, Texas	14.12	$169,495
Laredo, Texas	14.05	$168,603
Kansas City, Missouri	13.86	$166,376
Columbus, Ohio	13.76	$165,104
Fort Wayne, Indiana	13.63	$163,523
San Antonio, Texas	13.34	$160,043
Indianapolis, Indiana	13.18	$158,161
El Paso, Texas	12.79	$153,486
Lubbock, Texas	12.78	$153,333
Baltimore, Maryland	12.43	$149,179
Milwaukee, Wisconsin	12.43	$149,146
Corpus Christi, Texas	12.14	$145,670
Pittsburgh, Pennsylvania	11.14	$133,622
Buffalo, New York	10.66	$127,862
Toledo, Ohio	9.68	$116,148
Memphis, Tennessee	9.53	$114,368
Cleveland, Ohio	8.31	$99,716
Detroit, Michigan	5.35	$64,194

As you can see, average prices across the nation can greatly affect whether you will be able to find a property that's worth the purchase price if you want to make it a rental. As an investor, you're always seeking to do better than the average.

To recap, the decision is yours on what criteria you establish to determine what a "viable rental" is to you and your situation. As a new investor, always remember rule #1, cash flow, and abide by it. If you fail to purchase a property that cash flows from day one, you're setting yourself up for failure. Buying a house that does not have the ability to make you money from day one is signing on hundreds of thousands of dollars' worth of debt in exchange for a pile of sticks and bricks. This makes you a real estate buyer, but not an investor. Know the difference!

The Neighborhood

Within a market, or MSA (Metropolitan Statistical Area), there are many neighborhoods. Great ones, good ones, not so good ones, and the ones in which you're more likely to see combat than if you were overseas. Neighborhoods can be up and coming, stable, or in decline. Ideally, we're looking for an up-and-coming neighborhood in a good part of town. We may not always get what we want, so it's important to analyze neighborhoods with eyes wide open for our own enjoyment as we occupy the property, but also with the aim of making a great long-term investment. There is a lot of "feel" to determining whether a neighborhood is right for you and a ripe pick for a long-term investment. However, there are certain metrics and analysis we can perform to apply a little science to our neighborhood search as well.

Neighborhood Feel

When I was selling real estate, I would advise my clients to visit the neighborhoods they were interested in at night, not just during the day when we were touring homes. Is it well lit? Are there individuals out running or walking dogs? Are there kids playing before the streetlights come on? Does it feel like home? Human intuition picks up on things that we often can't articulate. If you have a bad feeling or vibe, acknowledge it. Your subconscious is picking up on things that you can't quite put your finger on that you aren't comfortable with. Does it look like people take care of their properties, or are there a lot of properties with overgrown yards, junk in the yard or driveway, or a used car lot on site? Properties that are run down on the outside usually aren't great on the inside. What does that do to neighborhood property values when they eventually sell? This part of neighborhood analysis is how you feel, and only you can determine what feels right for you. Even when a neighborhood or block looks and feels great, there can be more to the story and that is where the science comes into play.

Neighborhood Science

This is an extreme example, but it happened, and it provides a real-life account of how important it is to dig into the science of a neighborhood.

I was out showing a nice young military family around several areas of town. They had just relocated from the other side of the country and wanted to get the lay of the land before dialing in on their preferred neighborhood, which is a smart strategy. We had narrowed the search down to a few great neighborhoods, but then "the perfect house" popped up in a neighborhood we had not researched as thoroughly. They decided they'd like a tour and we went out to take a look. The block was great, and the neighborhood had a nice quiet feel to it, with a park right across the street complete with playground, a pond, fountain, foot bridge, and all kinds of ducks and geese. Inside the house, every box on their criteria list received a checkmark. We'd found the one!

We conducted the home inspection several days later and there were no major issues. However, the husband wanted to back out of the purchase, and it was because of something he'd uncovered about the neighborhood. The issue was regarding his soon-to-be next door neighbor, in particular. Fortunately, he had conducted his due diligence on the neighborhood as well as on the property itself. He uncovered the fact that one of the occupants of the house next door was a sex offender of the worst kind. The report showed that he had been convicted of horrific crimes against children. The family that I represented, who was under contract to purchase the home next door to this monster, had two children under the age of 10.

The house was great, the neighborhood was great, but there was absolutely no way they were going through with the purchase in light of this new information. The seller was furious and threatened to sue for my clients' "earnest money deposit," but I knew they didn't have a leg to stand on legally.

I'd specifically written in the contract that "buyer may release contract during home inspection period (7 days) for any reason or no reason at all and be refunded their EMD." Ultimately, I think the seller and the listing agent knew who was living next door, but there is no way to prove it.

My clients dodged a huge bullet because of their own diligence and determination to obtain all of the facts about the property and the surrounding area during their due diligence period. I implore you to do the same! Here is a great resource for a variety of information about neighborhoods all over the country, specifically the sex offender registry:

www.city-data.com

It is also a good idea to search for general crime as well to get an idea of what is going on in and around your neighborhood:

www.crimemapping.com

Neighborhood Amenities

It's important to know who is included in your prospective renter pool and to know this before you purchase. People are people, so the amenities and features of a neighborhood that you enjoy and played a part in your selection of a particular property will likely also play a part in your future tenants' decision of where they prefer to rent. What is attracting you to the neighborhood other than the structure of the house itself? Is it in a great school district for your kids? Even if you do not have children, schools are an important consideration for many future tenants, do not dismiss their importance in your property search criteria. How close are you to a major grocery store? Are there parks or recreation centers within the neighborhood or nearby? Does the neighborhood feature many options for dining and nightlife?

By no means are the questions above an exhaustive list. Neighborhoods are almost like living things, constantly changing, sometimes growing, sometimes decaying. It is important to look at the neighborhood and what's around it to get the entire picture. To get the best idea of where a neighborhood fits within the big picture, we need to widen our aperture and take a look at the market as a whole.

The MSA (Metropolitan Statistical Area)

Why do people use Facebook?

Seeing photos of your friend vacations? Debating politics? Memes? Cat videos? Quizzes that tell you what kind of animal you would be? Checking (and hoping) that your Ex's new significant other is not as good as you? All that is fine and well, but the reason people use Facebook... is because people... use Facebook. It's that simple. Without other people, the functions of the platform would be useless.

Analyzing a real estate market is surprisingly similar. Perhaps the reason people select housing is because there's a Starbucks next door, or it's because of the proximity to work, or to the park. The Starbucks, the jobs, and the community services arrived because of the people, which in turn, brings more people. Does that make sense? Let's take a look at a few key metrics that help stack the odds in our favor when selecting where to buy property.

Population:

People, people, people. People! Using our VA Loans, we are the first occupants of our investment under our ownership, but we probably won't be the last. When selecting a property, we obviously want it to be conducive to our own needs, but also need to look ahead to see what would make it a win for future tenants. If the population of the area you're considering is in steady decline, that's bad news. No matter how great your property is, there will be many options (more housing than those needing housing, simple supply vs demand) and you'll be on the wrong side of that equation. We want to look at areas that are experiencing population growth, not decline.

- **Jobs**: Is the military base the only employer? If so, it might not be the right market in which to buy a home. If your base is constantly on the chopping block to be shut down, and there is no other industry in town, that's a recipe for disaster.

- **New industry**: What large businesses are operating in the market other than the military?
- **Education**: Higher education provides fuel for various other industries to thrive, a college or university in the market is always a good thing.
- **Hospitals**: Health care is big business. Being close to a major medical center is another example of a recession resistant employer.

House Values, Rent Amounts

Everyone got crushed in 2008 if they were in the real estate market. Massive fortunes that were accumulated over the years, especially from 2000-2007, were obliterated. Since 2008, housing prices have risen steadily as a part of the best and longest recovery since The Great Depression. Many experts and novices alike are saying that the current Bull (rising) Market has gotten out of hand, and we face impending doom. I don't have a crystal ball, and suspect you don't either. What I do know, is that once we put the forces of real estate to work for us, it is the most powerful wealth building vehicle available.

The "equity" (or lack thereof) in a piece of property is only realized during a liquidation event (refinance or sale). If you do it right, you will have a much higher probability of weathering any future unforeseen storms in the economic cycles. Appreciation is the icing on the wealth cake, and while we don't count on it, it's very sweet when we do get some. With that in mind, it is wise to look back at what has been in terms of housing values. Look all the way back to the year 2000, or even before. See how the homes in your market responded in 2008, look how they have recovered since. Your real estate agent can help you with this data through their access to the Multiple Listing Service. Ideally, you are purchasing in a market that is trending upward in both property value as well as rent, which is a function of population and income.

Income:

We started off talking about people, and they truly are the key to this business, but there is another critically important factor: their ability to pay. As active duty military members, it's fairly easy to figure out what we and those like us can bring to the table as renters economically. Our Basic Allowance for Housing (BAH) adjusts annually, usually keeping up with inflation and taking other economic variables into consideration to ensure service members will be able to be able to obtain safe housing proximate to base. When we look at civilians, it's a more complicated process. We want to take a hard look at the data and trends to ensure that renters will be willing and able to move in when we change station or move into our next property.

Military tenants can be great. We all took the same oath and, on some level, look out for one another. As we all know, there are some who will not get their act together, and if we rent to them there will be problems. The good news is that we will have the contact to their Admin Department as a part of their lease. With this information, we will be able to obtain recourse on them in the event that they do not fulfill their obligations or damage our property. A possible downside of renting to military is that we know they will be leaving, it's just a question of when. Turnover costs (cleaning, repairs, marketing, and most importantly vacancy) in between tenants can really add up. Military tenants are also able to break their lease without charge in the event of a PCS or deployment. Whether you elect to rent to other military members or civilians is a personal choice with pros and cons on both sides. The most pressing question we have to address is, will the income from renting the property cover all of our expenses and provide cash flow every month?

There is an inverse relationship between how much cash flow we can derive on a particular property and it's purchase price. Generally, the lower the price of the property, the higher cash flow we will receive on a percentage basis. The conventional wisdom is that a person or household should spend about 30% of their income on housing (rent or mortgage) as part of a proper budget. In order to cater to the widest range of potential tenants, we want to be in the fat part of the bell curve within our particular market. It will vary by market, but nationally a good rule of thumb is to cater to tenants with average household incomes of $45,000-$60,000. The market you are analyzing might be higher in the case of a major metropolitan area, or lower in a smaller city.

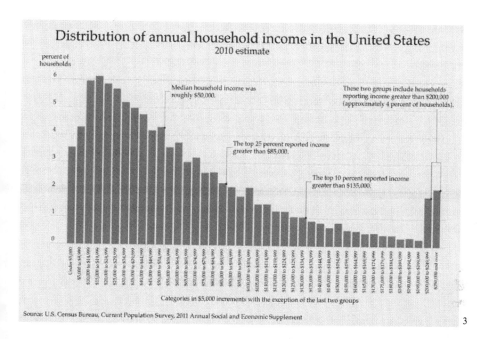

In addition to looking at average household income for an area, you will also want to search for rentals that are similar to your property in order to see how your property compares. In order to service the $45,000-$60,000 households operating within a normal budget, their optimal rental budget will be between $1,100-1,750. After reviewing the available rental comparables and analyzing the expenses you face with owning and maintaining the property, make sure you are comfortable with the likely spread between the market rent and your expenses. If the cash flow isn't as exciting as you'd hoped right off the bat, fear not! Remember that when you purchase the property, you lock in your "rent" for the next 30 years. As your tenants' income (or your BAH) goes up every year, your mortgage payment remains the same, your spread will continue to grow, and at the end of 30 years, you own it!

---

[3] Created by user *vikjam*, via Wikipedia Commons [CC BY-SA 3.0 (https://creativecommons.org/licenses/by-sa/3.0)]:
https://commons.wikimedia.org/wiki/File:Distribution_of_Annual_Household_Income_in_the_United_States_2010.png

Now you know how the VA Loan process works, you understand the power of owning real estate over time, you know what team members you need to be successful, what you're looking for in a property, how to obtain a discount, how to strategically add value to a property in order to create equity, how to analyze a neighborhood and market, and you're ready to buy your first property using your VA Loan. You may understand all of these concepts and be eager to learn more as you start your real estate journey, but still be wondering "how can this make me a millionaire?" The purpose of this book is to enable you to understand the basics and encourage you to take action. In typical military fashion, we're crawling to start. In the next section, we'll move on to a walk and ultimately a run. How far you wish to take your real estate journey is up to you!

Chapter Seven:

Advanced Strategies for Your VA Loan

House Hacking

While people have been employing this concept for many years, the term "House Hacking" was coined by the host of Bigger Pockets Podcast, Brandon Turner. If you haven't heard of Bigger Pockets, crawl out from under the rock you've been living under and check it out www.biggerpockets.com . House Hacking is a great example of pure American ingenuity. Basically, the goal of House Hacking is to reduce or eliminate one's own housing expenses by any means necessary. We've already established how you can generate massive long-term wealth by simply living in a house you purchase with your 0% down VA Loan, renting it when you leave and paying off the mortgage note over time. What if you could make (or save) a significant amount of money while occupying your primary residence? That's the beauty of House Hacking.

I purchased my first property using my VA Loan in 2010, about a year after arriving in Norfolk, VA. Fundamentally, real estate has always appealed to me, but I wasn't sure why. After reading Robert Kiyosaki's *Rich Dad Poor Dad,* I knew I needed to purchase a property of my own, especially since I could do so with 0% down. I didn't understand the concepts I'm writing about in this book in 2010, but fortunately I was saved by the market, a decent instinct on what value is, and ultimately a loyalty to a few of my buddies I went through SWCC training with.

When we arrived at Naval Amphibious Base Little Creek, we decided it would make sense to get a 3-bedroom apartment to reduce living costs for all three of us (the basis of house hacking). Very shortly thereafter, I was on the hunt for properties. Without knowing what I was doing, I actually created pretty good criteria for my purchase.

- There had to be enough bedrooms for both of my apartment roommates plus one other guy, so a total of four.
- It had to be within 10 minutes of base.
- It had to have a garage.
- It had to be purchased at a discount from fair market.

You'll notice some parallels from my novice criteria and the criteria I recommend in the chapter on selecting and analyzing properties. Basically, I was successful in achieving the following, which are key elements to a successful house hack:

- Extra space to monetize (three extra bedrooms and a garage).
- Desirable location.
- A discount from fair market on purchase cost as well as a spread between monthly liability (payments) and monthly monetization efforts (rent).

After a couple months of meticulous searching with several real estate agents (see the chapter on building your team), I finally found the right agent who "got it." He owned properties himself and had worked with dozens of active-duty service members, a lot of whom were in the Naval Special Warfare community and recommended him highly. Fortunately, before we started working together, I had already narrowed down my submarket and was very clear on my criteria. Here is how the deal worked out:

List Price	$275,000
Purchase Price	$250,000
Appraisal Value	$275,000
Closing Cost Assistance	$10,000

That ten grand paid for all of my loan costs, plus $2,000 of credit card debt, and I was able to get my $1,000 earnest money deposit back at closing!

Real estate appraisers got in a lot of trouble in the last crash. They were blamed along with the banks for enabling bad loans by valuing properties higher than they should have been. I was fortunate to receive an appraisal 10% higher than my purchase price. At the end of the day, having a higher appraisal doesn't do anything for you at purchase other than make you feel like you've got a good deal. The "fair market" or appraised value of the property only really matters if you're going for a refinance or selling the property. Because appraisers have been gun shy after the last crash, it is fairly common for the appraiser to value a property for the VA exactly at purchase price, which is why it's important to know how to analyze the numbers yourself and alongside your real estate agent to make sure you're walking in with "equity" as recommended in this book. Here's how the monthly numbers worked for this property:

Master Bedroom	Me!
In-law Suite	$800

Bedroom 3	$600
Bedroom 4	$600
Total Rent	**$2,000**
-Monthly Payment (PITI)	-$1,350
-Utilities	-$400
Cash Flow	**$250**

That's right, I purchased a $250,000 property at a 10% discount from fair market value, moved three of my buddies in, lived for free, AND collected an additional $3,000 per year. I'm sure there are others who have done it better, but this is a House Hacking homerun! What made the deal even better is that instead of living in a spare bedroom to create more cash flow, I had the huge master with the palatial bathroom including tile shower and jetted tub, and was getting paid to do it. Furthermore, with our deployment rotation, it was a rare event to have more than two roommates at home at the same time.

Remember the garage that was a "must have" on my criteria list? I was able to build out storage there and help other buddies store things who didn't live with me and were breaking their leases to go on deployment, without having to deal with the headache of a self-storage facility. I hadn't considered that as a possible revenue source when I purchased the property, I just knew I wanted a garage for my own use. I have heard of other military members who store cars for their buddies on deployment and start them up every couple of weeks to keep them running well. The essence of House Hacking is being creative and taking a path that is slightly harder than the default and using good old-fashioned American ingenuity to maximize the value of your property. Here are some other ways Veterans are maximizing their properties:

Small Multifamily

Most people use their VA Loan to buy a single-family home, townhome, or condo. Have you ever heard of a Duplex, Triplex, or Quad? You can purchase these types of properties with a VA Loan as well. Duplexes, Triplexes, and Quads enable you to househack, without having to worry about your roommates' dirty dishes or other undesirable behavior, because there's a wall separating you!

- **Duplex**: 2 attached residential units
- **Triplex**: 3 attached residential units
- **Quadruplex**: 4 attached residential units

The great thing about the three types of small multifamily properties, is that they are considered by the banks (and the VA) to be "residential property." Five units and up are considered "commercial properties" and different rules apply. The most applicable rule to our purposes is that VA Loans may not be used to purchase commercial properties.

When I was conducting my search in 2010, there was a Quadruplex a couple blocks away from the house I ultimately purchased that was on my list, but I decided against purchasing. Let's take a look at how it's performed relative to my property.

2010:

Quadruplex		My House	
Purchase Price	$250,000	*Purchase Price*	$250,000
Mortgage Payment	$1,350	*Mortgage Payment*	$1,350

Market Rent (¾ units)	$1,950	Roommates' Rent	$2,000
Expenses	$600	Expenses	$400
Monthly Cash Flow	**$0**	**Monthly Cash Flow**	**$250**

2019:

Quadruplex		**My House**	
Market Value	$300,000	Market Value	$330,000
Mortgage Payment	$1,350	Mortgage Payment	$1,350
Market Rent (all units)	$3,200	Rent (entire unit)	$2,000
Expenses	$1,000	Expenses	$400
Monthly Cash Flow	**$850**	**Monthly Cash Flow**	**$250**

There are a few interesting observations that can be made between my house and the quad that I passed up. What stuck out to you? Was any of this information surprising? Ultimately, both properties have performed well over the last decade, and I would have achieved my "house hacking" goal with the Quad as well. I elected to have the potential inconvenience of having roommates occupying the same space as me, and that generated an additional $250/mo. in cash flow versus the Quad. My house has also appreciated at a higher rate due to high demand for similar properties in the neighborhood.

The Quad pulled ahead when I moved out, however. With the fourth unit available for rent upon my departure, as well as a 3% average rent growth over the years, the Quad is now able to pull in $3,200 in gross rent every month compared to the house's $2,000. The Quad's expenses are also higher, but it still pulls ahead with $850 in cash flow every month versus my house's $250. What would you do with an extra $10,000 in cash flow every year? For most people, that's a significant amount of money!

Small multifamily properties are a coveted asset type among residential real estate investors, so expect stiff competition if you decide to pursue one for your first or next purchase. Just like any other asset type, deals can be created by taking advantage of inefficient markets, negotiating well, and ultimately… solving problems others are unwilling to tackle. A creative way many of my colleagues have overcome a difficult market for acquisitions and producing cash flow through traditional methods is by riding the wave of a new phenomenon, short-term rentals.

AirBnB & Short-Term Rentals

When I was a kid, my parents told me not to talk to strangers and to absolutely never get in their car. Fast forward 25 years, and just about everyone hops into a stranger's car fairly regularly while using a rideshare app. The shared economy is here, and that includes housing! An industry that was crafted around vacation rentals is now big business in many areas of the country. Being close to a military base, there will often be family and friends visiting their service members from out of town, folks PCSing in town to check out their long-term housing options, contractors and vendors working on base, and other likely travelers passing through. So even if there is no traditional vacation component to your area, hosting a short-term rental may be a viable strategy to create some additional cash flow.

You can utilize the short-term rental strategy are by either renting a room within your property, or renting the entire property. If you purchase a duplex, triplex, or quad, you have the luxury of doing short-term rental without actually interacting with your guests. I have military friends who are executing on all of the above strategies with great success, as well as nonmilitary friends who host hundreds of units at the enterprise level. Short-term rentals have taken the market by storm and are now big business. Whether this strategy is right for you or not is an individual decision. In some markets it's possible to achieve great nightly rates and it is worth figuring out

Phil Capron

the systems to capitalize on this phenomenon. A good place to check out the viability of short-term rentals for your market is listed below:

www.airdna.co

Chapter Eight:

Growing Your Portfolio and Achieving Financial Freedom

Purchasing one property with your VA Loan can do wonders for your financial outlook over time, but it is likely not enough to secure financial freedom for you and your family. The example of the Quad that I didn't buy only generates about $10,000 per year in cash flow. Don't get me wrong, that's a lot of money... but it's not financial freedom money. Most people are going to require much more than that to quit their day job. Using your VA Loan is like a 101-level class in college; it's an introduction to the world of real estate. Once you've purchased your first property, you're just starting down the rabbit hole. How deep it goes is up to you.

The VA Loan is simply one tool in the toolbox, but there are many others. Because of the 0% down feature, the VA Loan is often the best option for younger borrowers that have just joined the workforce and may not have a lot of money saved up to utilize other loan products. However, as your portfolio grows, it is likely you'll want to employ other strategies to acquire additional property and maximize cash flow and equity build up. Here are a few of my favorites.

Refinance

One of the superpowers of real estate is the ability to leverage bank money at a very low rate, because banks love the security (collateral) that real estate provides. This enables us as real estate investors to strategically refinance our properties to achieve maximum return on our equity and grow our cash flow towards our ultimate goal of financial freedom. There are three types of refinance that are interesting to us as VA Loan purchasers.

Interest Rate Reduction Refinance Loan (IRRRL)

We are enjoying some of the lowest interest rates in history at the time of printing, so this is the least applicable refinance option in the current market climate. The basic premise of the Interest Rate Reduction Refinance Loan is that current rates are significantly lower than the current rate you have on your mortgage. Thus, if you utilize an IRRRL, you'll be able to save money every month due to the lower payment. The drawback of this loan is that you are restarting the amortization (remember, the early years of a mortgage is a lot more "interest" than "principal").

You'll also be paying another round of "loan closing costs" either directly, or they will be rolled into the amount on your mortgage. There may be a time and place for this type of refinance, but it is hard to imagine a lending climate in which rates are much lower than they are currently. For reference, here is a chart of the historical interest rates for residential real estate over the years:

Year	Lowest Rate	Highest Rate	Average Rate	Year	Lowest Rate	Highest Rate	Average Rate
2018	3.95%	4.94%	4.54%	2015	3.59%	4.09%	3.85%
2017	3.78%	4.30%	3.99%	2014	3.80%	4.53%	4.17%
2016	3.41%	4.32%	3.65%	2013	3.34%	4.58%	3.98%

Year	Lowest Rate	Highest Rate	Average Rate	Year	Lowest Rate	Highest Rate	Average Rate
2012	3.31%	4.08%	3.66%	1998	6.49%	7.22%	6.94%
2011	3.91%	5.05%	4.45%	1997	6.99%	8.18%	7.60%
2010	4.17%	5.21%	4.69%	1996	6.94%	8.42%	7.81%
2009	4.71%	5.59%	5.04%	1995	7.11%	9.22%	7.93%
2008	5.10%	6.63%	6.03%	1994	6.97%	9.25%	8.38%
2007	5.96%	6.74%	6.34%	1993	6.74%	8.07%	7.31%
2006	6.10%	6.80%	6.41%	1992	7.84%	9.03%	8.39%
2005	5.53%	6.37%	5.87%	1991	8.35%	9.75%	9.25%
2004	5.38%	6.34%	5.84%	1990	9.56%	10.67%	10.13%
2003	5.21%	6.44%	5.83%	1989	9.68%	11.22%	10.32%
2002	5.93%	7.18%	6.54%	1988	9.84%	10.77%	10.34%
2001	6.45%	7.24%	6.97%	1987	9.03%	11.58%	10.21%
2000	7.13%	8.64%	8.05%	1986	9.29%	10.99%	10.19%
1999	6.74%	8.15%	7.44%	1985	11.09%	13.29%	12.43%

Phil Capron

Year	Lowest Rate	Highest Rate	Average Rate
1984	13.14%	14.68%	13.88%
1983	12.55%	13.89%	13.24%
1982	13.57%	17.66%	16.04%
1981	14.80%	18.63%	16.64%
1980	12.18%	16.35%	13.74%
1979	10.38%	12.90%	11.20%
1978	8.98%	10.38%	9.64%
1977	8.65%	9.00%	8.85%
1976	8.70%	9.10%	8.87%
1975	8.80%	9.60%	9.05%
1974	8.40%	10.03%	9.19%
1973	7.43%	8.85%	8.04%
1972	7.23%	7.46%	7.38%
1971	7.29%	7.73%	7.54%

VA to Conventional Refinance

An amazing benefit of a VA Loan is fact that no Private Mortgage Insurance is required, which saves us as VA borrowers hundreds of dollars a month, and tens of thousands over the life of our ownership. Conventional loans require an equity position of at least 20% in order to waive the requirement for PMI. On a modest $200,000 house, $40,000 in equity is required in order to be exempt from the private mortgage insurance. If you want to cut a check for that amount, good for you. I personally do not wish to do so. That is why this book is not just about buying properties, but buying properties properly! If you purchase a property properly with at least a 10% equity position the day you close you are already halfway to the required 20% equity position needed to refinance into a Conventional Loan with no PMI required. After purchase you may elect to force appreciation and create additional sweat equity by addressing unsightly cosmetic issues. With this combination of negotiated equity and forced appreciation, along with a stable or slightly appreciating market, you'll be able to execute a VA to Conventional Refinance with little or no money out of pocket at the refinance closing after a few years of ownership.

Now that we've freed up our VA entitlement, we're free to leapfrog into the next house with 0% down, rinse, and repeat. This is essentially the same strategy employed by many real estate investors. Our goal is to maximize our cash on cash return or "return on investment" (ROI). Bigger Pockets Podcast host Brandon Turner coined an acronym for this strategy that is now in common parlance in the investor world. He calls it the "BRRRR Method" which stands for

- Buy
- Rehab
- Rent
- Refinance
- Repeat

In order to employ this strategy as a non-veteran, a person must either save up the cash to purchase the property or use a Conventional or Renovation loan.

Even in the case of a Conventional or Renovation loan, there are significant out of pocket costs to the investor. Simply put, this strategy requires money to get started. The beauty of the VA Loan is that we don't need to have tremendous resources in order to make real estate work for us. Instead of having a bunch of money in a bank account, we are creating it through our hard work, ingenuity, and the fantastic tool that is the VA Loan.

Eventually, our efforts will allow that money to flow into our bank accounts! You can be as aggressive as you want to be with this strategy, but let's take a look at an example of someone who purchased their first property with 2 years of active duty service and repeated the process every 4 years over the course of their military career. We will assume a refinance amount of $200,000 (80% of $250,000) and an interest rate of 5%, and a market appreciation rate of 2%. Let's see how this would work over a 20-year military career.

House Number	Year Purchased	Years Amortized	Amortization	Appreciation	**Total**
1	2020	14	$64,000	$70,000	$134,000
2	2024	10	$42,000	$50,000	$92,000
3	2028	6	$24,000	$30,000	$54,000
4	2032	2	$6,000	$10,000	$16,000
5	2036	0	VA	Loan	$50,000
					$544,000

Pretty amazing, isn't it? With this one tactic, it is possible to amass over half a million dollars over 20 years on a military salary! Some of your smart Air Force folks might wonder how the total equity equals $544,000. Don't forget, in order to refinance from VA to Conventional, we needed to have a 20% equity position. The first 4 properties on the list were refinanced with $50,000 of equity already in place. The chart above shows what has occurred through amortization (it's just math) and a very modest appreciation rate of 2% (which isn't even compounded) for illustrative purposes. The VA to Conventional Refinance is just one tool in our VA Loan tool box, but it certainly is a useful one!

VA Cash Out Refinance

Some of you might be saying "all of that equity is great... but what does it actually do for me? I can't spend it." You're absolutely right. Equity in properties will increase your Net Worth, but what does that actually do for you other than allow you to sleep well at night? Not much. Having a high Net Worth combined with good credit will assist you in obtaining loans on bigger real estate deals or other assets, but net worth alone does not put money in your pocket. Fortunately, with a VA Loan, you are eligible to "Cash Out Refinance" for 100% of your properties' appraised value. It is exactly what it sounds like, let's use my property as an example. I purchased it in 2010 for $250,000. Since then, I've paid off $30,000 of principal though amortization. My appraisal in 2010 came in at $275,000, and the current appraised value is $330,000, so I've also enjoyed the benefit of appreciation due to a strong real estate market and local demand.

Current Appraised Value	$330,000
- Current Mortgage Balance	-$220,000
Equity Position	$110,000

As with most things in this business, there are costs incurred with this strategy. The first and most obvious is that your mortgage payment will go up every month due to the additional debt incurred. It is important to make sure that the new mortgage payment is comfortable before executing a Cash Out Refinance. The amount of closing costs will vary based on your situation. The good news is most of the closing costs incurred with a Cash Out Refinance can be rolled into the new loan. For my situation above let's assume the closing costs are $10,000. I'd still be walking away from the closing table with a check for $100,000, for something I did nine years ago, that has made me every month between then and now. I would be pretty happy about that! The only "catch" is that you have to occupy the property at the time of refinance if you wish to receive cash back from the transaction.

The next important question for my situation is "what should be done with the $100,000 cash?" This money is tax free, because it is additional "debt" on my balance sheet, as opposed to ordinary or investment income that would be taxed. Ultimately, the decision is up to me, and a lot rides on my decision. Ideally, I should choose to reinvest this tax-free money into other assets. Many people made the mistake of taking equity out of their houses in the mid 2000's only to spend that money on junk, and they paid a heavy price as a result. The key in this business is to leverage your cash and equity in assets in order to buy other assets. As you may have guessed, my favorite types of assets are real estate assets!

Investing in Residential Real Estate

We're talking about equity we've earned through the strategic use of our VA Loan eligibility in this book, but if you are still on active duty, there are a couple other ways you could obtain a significant amount of cash.

- Signing/ reenlistment bonuses
- Deployment money

Are you the one who comes home from an overseas tour and drops all of that cash on a new car, bike, or boat? If so, I hope that stops after reading this book. There is a better way! All of those toys, while nice to have and fun to play with, are liabilities... they don't make us money now and they never will. Investing in real estate allows us to grow our wealth and allow others to pay for our toys.

Since you have your first purchase under your belt, the idea of going from a crawl (buying your own house) to a walk (buying a rental house) shouldn't be too overwhelming. The real estate concepts you've learned so far all still apply. The difference in your first investment purchase is that you will be using conventional financing and that you will be using a sizeable chunk of your own money. The goal is still to allow other people (renters) to pay down (loan amortization) your cash flowing, appreciating, and tax advantageous real property. Instead of using our hard-earned deployment money, reenlistment bonus, or equity cashed out from a successful VA Loan purchase for a toy, let's see what it would do for us if we took $40,000 and deployed it into a well purchased single family home.

We could purchase a modest single-family home for $150,000 using a 20% down payment of $30,000 and $10,000 for cosmetic improvements to the property. The mortgage of $120,000 at a 5% interest rate has a payment of $644/mo. for Principal and Interest. Taxes, Insurance, property management fees, and repair reserves will vary and be extra. For the sake of round numbers, let's say that our total monthly cost is $1,200/mo. and it is a 1% deal (do you remember the calculation?) meaning that the rent is $1,500/mo., 1% of the purchase price of $150,000. This example property would generate $300/mo. in cash flow. Would that amount of money be able to lease or finance the toy many service members pay cash for? More importantly, from an investment standpoint, is it a good use of our cash to purchase this property?

$300/mo. x 12= $3,600/year

$3,600/ $40,000 cash invested = 9% annual cash on cash return

A 9% cash on cash return on top of all of the other wealth building forces real estate owners enjoy sounds like a pretty good deal to me! If the $300/mo. isn't enough to get you excited, perhaps a small multifamily property would be a better option for you. Duplexes, Triplexes, and Quads are considered to be residential real estate from the bank's perspective, but they have the ability to generate more cash flow than their single-family counterparts because there are multiple tenants. In addition to providing more income, additional units also provide an element of security by spreading the risk associated with owning and managing property across several tenants.

If a single-family property goes vacant, or has a problem tenant, 100% of the rental income is lost during that period. In the case of a Quadruplex, one bad tenant costs us 25% of the rental income until the problem is corrected. In this business, the more units we have, the better it is for our long-term wealth building. Perhaps you like the idea of owning real estate for all of the great advantages we've discussed in this book, but the idea or managing them all yourself or even being responsible for managing the property manager makes you uncomfortable. Multifamily real estate might be a solution for you!

Multifamily Real Estate

From my bio you probably get the idea that I like multifamily real estate, or apartments. I like them, I like them a lot. Larger commercial buildings enjoy the same benefits described previously as they pertain to residential real estate. However, not everyone wants to run apartment buildings at an enterprise level like I do. On the other side of the spectrum, some people don't want to manage single family properties or be responsible for managing the property managers. Fortunately, there is a way for people to own pieces of larger commercial properties "passively."

Unlike single family homes, it is uncommon for an individual to own a large apartment complex. Usually, they are owned by corporations or by small partnerships of people like me. I have some great partnerships with other veterans who used their VA Loan to get started, kept buying houses throughout their career, and eventually decided to use the equity and cash they'd accrued over the years to do bigger projects. I know even more people who don't wish to be a part of the management team on apartment buildings, but want their money working for them through real estate. They are our "passive investors" or "limited partners." Basically, the limited partners take a look at the deal we are raising money to purchase, or have an existing relationship with us and know about our proven track record, and decide to invest their money, but allow us as the operations team to captain the ship. This enables the limited partners to own part of a large building, without any of the headaches associated with the day to day management.

If the idea of larger projects interests you, I'd encourage you to educate yourself thoroughly before considering an investment of this type, it's certainly not for everyone. Here is a link to the group I work with closely helping new investors purchase their first apartment building. There is a lot of free information if you think apartment buildings might be a part of your real estate journey:

www.themichaelblank.com

Apartment buildings are awesome, small multifamily is great, racking up single family homes is good. Real estate investing is kind of like dieting or working out, the diet or workout that works... is the one that you do. If you decide that buying a house for you and your family is as far as you wish to take your real estate journey, you'll still be light years ahead of your peers that elect to rent for their entire lives. I point out other real estate strategies not as a recommendation that you should dive right in, but because most people don't understand that these opportunities exist. The key is to get started and use your VA Loan on the right opportunity as quickly as possible. As you've learned so far, the wider you can make the base of your real estate pyramid, the better. I didn't start by buying 100 apartments, I started with one relatively modest single-family home. You can start that way as well. That one decision I made while on active duty has created over $100,000 in equity in less than a decade in that one property and opened the door for me to create millions more across the rest of my portfolio, all because of my VA Loan.

Real estate is not a get rich quick scheme that might work if you get lucky. Real estate is a vehicle to become incredibly wealthy over time, for certain. The catch is that real estate can't start working for you until you get off the fence and get in the game. The earlier you get started, the longer the forces of real estate wealth building are able to conspire on your behalf to make you very wealthy and financially free, if that's what you want.

Phil Capron

Chapter Nine:

Keep Your Grit

"I CAN IMAGINE NO MORE REWARDING A CAREER. AND ANY MAN WHO MAY BE ASKED IN THIS CENTURY WHAT HE DID TO MAKE HIS LIFE WORTHWHILE, I THINK CAN RESPOND WITH A GOOD DEAL OF PRIDE AND SATISFACTION: 'I SERVED IN THE UNITED STATES NAVY." JFK

The VA Loan is an amazing benefit that we as veterans can enjoy to make a home for ourselves and our families. The GI Bill enables us to write our own ticket regarding our access to higher education. We've shared experiences that bond us with our teammates for life. We should all sleep well at night and hold our heads high knowing that we did things that the overwhelming majority of our countrymen couldn't or wouldn't do to ensure our continued freedom and preservation of our way of life. These are all great benefits of service, but I believe there is one that is often overlooked that may be the most valuable.

In our education system and in much of our society at large, the opportunity to truly learn has been snuffed out. An unintended consequence of standardized testing designed to "leave no child behind" and sports teams whose mission isn't to win, but to treat everyone equally regardless of skill. The theory is that failure and loss is too painful to be dealt with, and should be avoided at all costs. We all served in the military... we understand failure and loss in ways that the rest of the population never will, and I believe that is our greatest strength.

In boot camp, SWCC training, pre deployment work ups, technical schools, and ultimately at the review board that ended my Navy career... winning was never an option, I just didn't realize it at the time. If you look back on your military career, I'm sure you can recall times in which you were put in unwinnable situations. Did you realize they were unwinnable and quit? Unlikely, especially if your situation was on the battlefield.

It is the repeated exposure to the unwinnable that makes us unstoppable. We've learned how to fail and how to lose over and over again, by design. What most of the civilian population and the big brains in charge of the education system fail to realize is that these failures aren't fatal. They train us to keep striving for a solution with every fiber of our being, because quitting isn't an option. We also debrief and figure out what went wrong so we can do it better next time, instead of hiding from failure and pretending it never happened. This exposure to adversity and failure calluses our mind according to David Goggins in his book *Can't Hurt Me*. He's made it his life's mission to see how far he can push himself in every area of life.

Angela Duckworth studied this concept and published her findings in great detail in her book *Grit*. Early in the book she follows the "Plebes" at the United States Military Academy at West Point trying to figure out why some persevere and conquer training, while others fall by the wayside or quit. Her findings mirrored my own less than scientific study immersed in the chilly waters of the Pacific Ocean at Naval Special Warfare Basic Training Command. I watched guys stronger, faster, and smarter than me succumb to the pressure and quit. They couldn't overcome the societal doctrine that failure is fatal.

Phil Capron

> *"Failures are going to happen, and how you deal with them may be the most important thing in whether you succeed. You need fierce resolve. You need to take responsibility. You call it grit. I call it fortitude. The ultimate thing is that we need to grow over time. Demonstrate determination, resiliency, and tenacity. Do not let temporary setbacks become permanent excuses. And, finally, use mistakes and problems as opportunities to get better - not reasons to quit."*
>
> *~ Jamie Dimon, from <u>Grit</u> by Angela Duckworth*

As veterans, we all have this "grit" in our guts. It's important that we don't forget it. When I went through "TAPS," or "Transitional Assistance Program" on my way out of the Navy, I didn't make it past the first day. The retired E-9 teaching the fifty or so transitioning sailors kept bragging about his 100% permanent and total disability rating and I thought to myself "wait... didn't you say you worked in admin and spent your entire career behind a desk?" If you're hurt, you're hurt, but it certainly made me raise an eyebrow knowing many of my guys with denied claims for injuries sustained downrange or on high risk training ops.

As he continued through his presentation and arrived at the various ailments that you could claim disability for and "there was no way for the doctor to disprove it" I got my things together, stood up, and walked out. The genesis of this book came to me early in my real estate sales career when I realized how much malpractice was going on in real estate sales and lending... because the service members and veterans didn't know enough about the subject to protect themselves and their interests. However, as the years passed and my real estate portfolio grew, I realized that there was an even higher purpose for writing this. I cannot in good conscience sit idly by and allow people like that asshole from TAPS to poison our service members minds. He wants you to think that you are weak, broken, and that you can't do anything when you separate from service. I want you to remember that you are strong, gritty, enterprising, and that you can do anything when you separate from service. While my statement stands on its own, having money certainly helps open doors for your post service "anything."

Real estate isn't a special ops selection course, it's not West Point, and it's certainly not comparable to being downrange. It's just a game. A winnable game. Everything covered in this book has been done before thousands and thousands of times by people no smarter and no better than you. The key to success is figuring out what winning means to you, and as soon as possible, to chart a course of how to get to the winner's circle.

Chapter 10:

Your Big Why and Your Big Who

I don't know who first introduced the concept of the "Big Why" to business and pop culture, but it seems like a lot of people are talking about it, and for good reason. I was first introduced to the idea when I became a real estate agent with Keller Williams Realty shortly after separating from active duty in 2012. Gary Keller, author of several books including "The One Thing" and "The Millionaire Real Estate Investor," both of which I recommend highly, speaks often about finding your "Big Why." Another well-known author who is a proponent of the "Why" movement is Simon Sinek. His bestseller "Start with Why" posits that the "Why" is the core question to be addressed, only then can one move on to the "how" and "what." I think what both authors are saying is that, without a clear purpose, a person is likely to fold in the face of adversity. With a compelling why, or mission, they are more likely to proceed and thus succeed in whatever endeavor they are pursuing. Everyone has one. Even drug addicts.

I'm not trying to make light of a very sad and unfortunate situation affecting so many in our country, but drug addicts truly are some of the most successful people on earth. You're probably thinking that run ins with the law, potential homelessness, fractured relationships, and the awful health consequences of drug abuse don't exactly align with the image of success you've conjured in your mind.

I agree.

However, keep in mind that our image of success is not their image of success. Addiction has hijacked the brain of the addict to achieve a single mission, to get high. In that mission, if nothing else, the addict is a success. Their body and mind cannot tolerate anything less or they will face severe withdrawal symptoms. The addict will do anything to achieve their goal. They will beg, lie, cheat, steal, and even kill to fulfill their "why." Sad but true. It's an extreme example, and perhaps you're thinking that without the influence of powerful drugs there is no way for a normal person could apply that level of tenacity to achieving their goal, to fulfilling their "Big Why."

Let's take a look at the story of one of my mentors, Hal Elrod. He is the best-selling author of *The Miracle Morning,* which is essentially his thesis of how the most successful people in the world have particular morning routines. He interviewed, analyzed, and came up with a list of 6 of the most common practices among the mega successful and combined them into a powerful morning ritual that has transformed millions of lives across multiple continents. The world almost didn't receive this amazing work from Hal, as he died for several minutes after a drunk driver obliterated his Ford Mustang in a head on collision when he was 20 years old. When Hal woke up in the hospital, he found out he had over a dozen broken bones. He spent days in a coma, and upon regaining consciousness he had to face his new reality of likely never walking again or living a normal life, he had to decide how he was going to respond to his new reality.

The way he did had the doctors and hospital staff convinced that he had a screw loose. They all marveled that nobody who had experienced his level of trauma could possibly be so happy and engaging, unless they were delusional. The doctors sat Hal's parents down and explained their concerns, and asked if they would intercede and invite Hal to share how "he was really feeling." When confronted with the diagnosis of "delusional" by his father, Hal quickly set the record straight for everyone. He wasn't delusional, at all. He employed a strategy taught to him by his sales company called "the five-minute rule," which states that whenever something bad happens, you are entitled to five minutes to yell, scream, cry, stomp around, or whatever makes you feel better.

At the conclusion of the 5 minutes you say "can't change it" and proceed with life intelligently.

At 20 years old, Hal was understandably scared about the prospect of never walking again. Alone in his hospital room after visiting hours were over, he had a decision to make. He decided that if the diagnosis was correct and that he would never walk again, he was going to be the happiest person in a wheelchair anyone had ever encountered, but his big why was to walk again, and he set out a plan to take his first steps. Miraculously, his bones healed in record time, including a smashed femur, and the doctors allowed him to take his first steps a few short weeks after impact. Hal has gone on to do amazing things in life, you should pick up his books or go see him speak if you have the opportunity. He is the true definition of establishing his why and making it happen no matter what.

If you aren't sold on my examples of addicts who have had their brains hijacked by terrible drugs, or of a very exceptional human being in Hal Elrod, how about you? Because you're reading this, that makes you part of an elite fraternity comprising less than a tenth of the population of the United States. The numbers fluctuate, but less than half of one percent are serving on active duty at any given time, and less than 10% of the population has ever worn the uniform. About half of the veteran population is over the age of 60. If you are a post-Vietnam veteran, you are a volunteer… Why did you do it? Why did you sign on the dotted line? Were you seeking adventure? Facing jail time? In need of a steady paycheck? Looking for help with college? Do you bleed red, white, and blue? Why did you do it? Everyone has their reasons, but if you really dig in, I know you'll find a compelling Why that is uniquely yours.

This book is about real estate and using it as a vehicle to achieve financial freedom, even becoming a millionaire if that is important to you. So, financially, what is your Big Why? You picked up this book for a reason. Is it just to learn the mechanics of the VA Loan so you can buy one property and go back to your regular life? I don't think so. You've worked hard, you deserve nice things and to live the lifestyle of your dreams. Let's have some fun with this, shall we? Keep in mind, what one man can do… another can do. Nothing is off limits in this exercise. Get excited! Clarity on what you actually want is the first step towards obtaining it.

What do you want?

What would you have if you had a Genie granting you 5 new possessions? A new car? Boat? Guitar? What are your top 5?

1.

2.

3.

4.

5.

Phil Capron

Vacations: Where would you like to go?

Snowboarding in the Alps? A safari in South Africa? Hiking the Inca Trail at Machu Picchu? Seeing the Great Wall of China? Would these trips cost money? Absolutely. The greater cost of these adventures? Time. Most jobs don't allow for much time off, so if you're to achieve all of your dream vacations while you're still young enough to enjoy them, how? It's clear you want to create a life of time freedom and abundance, or you wouldn't have picked up this book. Just remember, if the why is big enough, the how will present itself. So, let your mind run wild. Where in the world would you like to go?

1.

2.

3.

4.

5.

6.

7.

8.

9.

10.

What would you like to do? What would you like to accomplish in your lifetime?

There is more to life than going to work, eating, and sleeping. How would you like to spend your time? Are you a football fanatic? How about season tickets for your favorite NFL or college team? Do you wish you had more time to fish and hunt? Would you like to coach your kids little league team but don't have the time? What would you most like to do if you didn't have to punch the clock for 40 hours or more every week to keep food on the table and a roof over your head? What are your top 10 things that you must accomplish in your lifetime?

1.

2.

3.

4.

5.

6.

7.

8.

9.

10.

I hope you set some big goals. This is your life, after all. As you learned from my story, anything is possible when you rule out defeat as an option and keep pressing forward. You don't have to be the best; you just have to figure out what you want and refuse to yield. Your VA Loan is an amazing tool to get you started in the wonderful world of real estate. So, what is it going to take monetarily to make everything on your list a reality? What is your number?

Do you remember when McDonalds released the Monopoly Game in the 90s? My buddies and I would scrounge up couch money or do odd jobs and ride our bikes into town to take our shot at the $1,000,000 top prize as often as we could. It seemed easy, just collect both Blue properties and voila, you get a million bucks. Upon reading the fine print, I discovered that once I collected the two Blue properties, I would actually have two options:

1. $1,000,000 in one lump sum

2. $50,000 per year for 20 years

Which one would you choose?

While $1,000,000 cash sounds pretty cool, is it? What would you do with it? Would you blow it all in year one and be back to where you started? Statistically, that's what happens to most lottery winners. I'd like to challenge you that you don't actually want $1,000,000 to blow, you'd rather have the dividends of what $1,000,000 conservatively invested would yield, year after year. Using the Monopoly example, if we had $1,000,000 invested in mutual funds or bonds that produced a 5% return annually, that's $50,000. What would you do with an extra $50,000 per year?

Investing is different than the McDonald's contest because if you had a 20-year bond on your $1,000,000, you'd get the $50,000 per year and then recoup your initial $1,000,000 at the end of the term. It's a pretty good deal, but the catch is that you have to have $1,000,000 to implement that plan. Through real estate, you can generate similar results over time, without having $1,000,000 in the bank to start with. Earlier in the book, I showed you how just using your VA Loan properly several times over the course of a military career can generate over $500,000 in real estate equity. That example doesn't even entertain redeploying the equity and cash flow created through your VA Loan purchases into additional real estate investments that create even more equity and cash flow for you.

The question you need to answer for yourself is, how much income do you need to generate passively to replace the income from your job and keep you living a lifestyle that is comfortable for you?

Monthly Passive Income:
$ _____

> *"We make a living by what we get, but we make a life by what we give"* -Winston Churchill

The concept of a big why is so powerful, and I'm glad it's gained so much popularity in our society in recent years. However, while I think the why is on the pulse of the most important, it is a near miss. The heart of what is most important to most of us isn't the why, but the who.

When I asked my best friend how he made it through Basic Underwater Demolition/SEAL training he admitted that there were some absolutely brutal times, guys were dropping like flies and quitting, accepting the bribe of a warm shower and some sleep in exchange for giving up on a dream they'd worked so hard to achieve (their why). He gave me a peek behind the curtain of what it takes to be successful in the midst of some of the most grueling military training in the world. The list of "why's" like patriotism, a paycheck, or adventure weren't going to cut it anymore. The "why" goes out the window, the "who" is the force that sustains you and gives you the strength to go on.

Looking through military history, I found that my best friend's BUD/S class was hardly unique. The history books are flush with examples of men and women doing things for their teammates that they wouldn't do for themselves. An unforgettable and heart wrenching example everyone should know is the story of Sergeant First Class Randy Shugart and Master Sergeant Gary Gordon in the battle of Mogadishu, Somalia.

After a Blackhawk was shot down in the city, these two Delta Force soldiers insisted they be dropped into the crash site to secure a perimeter, not even knowing if anyone was alive down there. They successfully repelled hordes of local militia members and killed a countless number of hostiles. Ultimately, they were successful and their actions saved the one surviving member of the crash, pilot Michael Durant. These men knew the prospects of getting out of there weren't good, but they did it anyway, sacrificing their own safety so that their wounded wouldn't be left defenseless and face certain slaughter.

At a conference recently, I was honored to meet Congressional Medal of Honor Winner Florent Groberg, Captain, US Army. He was the keynote speaker and I was surprised that he didn't share much about his commendation, but instead focused his speech on what all of us in the audience (veterans) had left to give to our communities and our country, and how we could best support one another as a military family. I was so impressed with how he sought to give back to other members of the military community that I looked up his story when I got home. He is a Congressional Medal of Honor Winner, so I shouldn't have been surprised when reading his commendation, but I was. Captain Groberg was leading a delegation of top US and Afghan forces to meet with village elders and was charged with securing their transit. They were ambushed by two suicide bombers and Captain Groberg charged and ultimately tackled one of the bombers after pushing him as far from the rest of his team and the high ranking officers as possible. He absorbed and deflected the blast upon detonation, saving countless lives.

Captain Groberg's actions were a direct reflection of his "big who." Even though he was the mission leader and an officer, he didn't hesitate and did what he had to do to save American lives. His men were his "big who." Because of Captain Groberg's commitment to them, many of their lives were saved that day.

Who are you fighting for? Who are you living for? The toys, vacations, and money are nice to have… but when you really think about it, I think that you'll realize most of those things don't mean much without the people who are most important to you. So, who are they? What are you willing to do for them? Pick your top 3 and write what is the most important thing you can do to make their life better. Hint: for children and significant others, love is spelled T I M E. When you stop to think about it, the "stuff" might not be as important to them as making it to a baseball game or making date night as scheduled.

1.

2.

3.

When I first started writing this book, the goal setting exercise was Chapter 3. I decided to move it, because all of the hopes and dreams in the world are conjured in vain without the tools required and the path to follow in order to reach them. It is my sincere hope that you can clearly see the path that's right for you and your life, or at the very least a few waypoints on your journey in real estate ownership. I hope that you took the time to write your goals and why they are important. Studies show that those with written goals are exponentially more likely to achieve them than those with a vague idea of what they want and no plan to make it happen.

If you skipped the goal setting exercise, please go back and complete it now, you'll be happy you did. Refer back to these goals often, they are what you actually want out of life, do not yield to obstacles and aggravations as they present themselves. Focus on the goal and the next actionable step to get there, and when you look back several years from now, you'll be able to see the path you've blazed with a lot more clarity than today when you planned it, because you've walked it.

Phil Capron

Postlogue:

Moving Forward

"Education without implementation is just entertainment" Rock Thomas

Obviously, I'm happy you decided to pick up my book. I hope that now that the curtain has been pulled back on the VA Loan and what it can do for you that you're ready to take massive action. Unfortunately, right now is the most motivated you will be to go after the goals you just wrote and all of the great intentions that are still trapped in your head. That's the paradox of additional education. It tricks you into thinking you're accomplishing great things, when in reality you haven't left the starting block. Ongoing education will be critical to your ultimate success, but do not become intoxicated with the feel good chemicals that come with learning. You actually have to do something! Here are a few educational resources that I believe will be helpful on your journey

Websites:

www.biggerpockets.com

Books:

Millionaire Real Estate Investor, by Gary Keller

Rich Dad Poor Dad, by Robert Kiyosaki

Tribe of Millionaires, by David Osborn, Pat Hiban, Mike McCarthy, and Tim Rhode

Podcasts:

Your VA Loan: with Phil Capron

> *If you've taken action and used your VA Loan, I'd love to have you on the show to share your success! Email me at* **podcast@philcapron.com**

From Military to Millionaire

Active Duty Passive Income

Bigger Pockets Podcast

If education makes you feel good, writing your goals will make you feel great! It is amazing to think of all that you could accomplish in life and put it on paper. Sadly, most people miss out on the pinnacle of achievement and the satisfaction that comes with setting a huge goal and making progress towards it every single day. Most people never think about them or set them to begin with, and most who do actually write them down never look at them again! Remember, at every inflection point in this book I've asked you to do a little bit more than the minimum required. You've done a great thing by setting your goals, now you need to honor them. Set an alarm on your phone to look at your goals every Sunday evening, that way you can make sure that your actions for the following week are representative of what you actually want in life.

If you want to have what others do not, to do what others cannot, and to be a person you can be proud of, you have to take the stairs when everyone else is riding the elevator. The stairs are a lot more fun when you've got somebody to talk to as you're climbing. It's also less likely you'll trip and fall. Because of that fact, I highly recommend you surround yourself with those who are also choosing to take the stairs. My entire life changed when I upleveled my peer group to include people who are where I want to go in life, and those on similar paths as my own. The first mastermind group I joined is called M1 which stands for "March to 1 Million." The mission of our group is to create "whole life millionaires" who are financially free, have great relationships, genuinely contribute to society, enjoy age defying health, and plan and participate in bucket list adventures.

www.gom1.com

A fantastic book illustrating the power of your peer group, written by the founders of another mastermind group I'm a part of called GoBundance is called "Tribe of Millionaires" and it is a fantastic parable about how your life changes when your peer group does. You can find out more about GoBudance here:

www.gobundance.com

Whether you treat this book as entertainment or the missing puzzle piece that completes the bridge towards an entirely different life is up to you. I'm not naive enough to think that this book is going to sell 1,000,000 copies or be the next "Rich Dad Poor Dad," however, I do know that this information can change the lives of some of my favorite people: my fellow veterans. I wasn't a very good sailor, but I'm pretty good at this real estate thing. I have a great life pursuing my passions and working towards my goals every day. The purpose of this book is to help you find, pursue, and obtain yours. It is with profound humility that I thank you for reading my book, for serving our great country, and for your willingness to continue to do so every day. If I can be of assistance to you in your journey, please let me know.

Very Respectfully,

Phil Capron